BUILDING**IDEAS**

BUILDING IDEAS

AN ARCHITECTURAL GUIDE TO THE UNIVERSITY OF CHICAGO

BY **JAY PRIDMORE**

PHOTOGRAPHS BY **TOM ROSSITER**

FOREWORD BY **ROBERT J. ZIMMER**

THE UNIVERSITY OF CHICAGO PRESS

CHICAGO AND LONDON

OPENING ILLUSTRATIONS

Harold Leonard Stuart Hall (title page)

Map of campus landmarks

Aerial view of the campus

Springtime in the humanities quad

Joseph Regenstein Library

Courtyard of the Reva and David Logan Center for the Arts

Charles M. Harper Center

The University of Chicago Press, Chicago 60637

The University of Chicago Press, Ltd., London

© 2013 by The University of Chicago

All rights reserved. Published 2013.

Printed in the United States of America

22 21 20 19 18 17 16 15 14 13   1 2 3 4 5

ISBN-13: 978-0-226-04680-8 (paper)

A cataloging-in-publication record for this book is available at the Library of Congress.

∞ This paper meets the requirements of ANSI/NISO Z39.48-1992 (Permanence of Paper).

CONTENTS

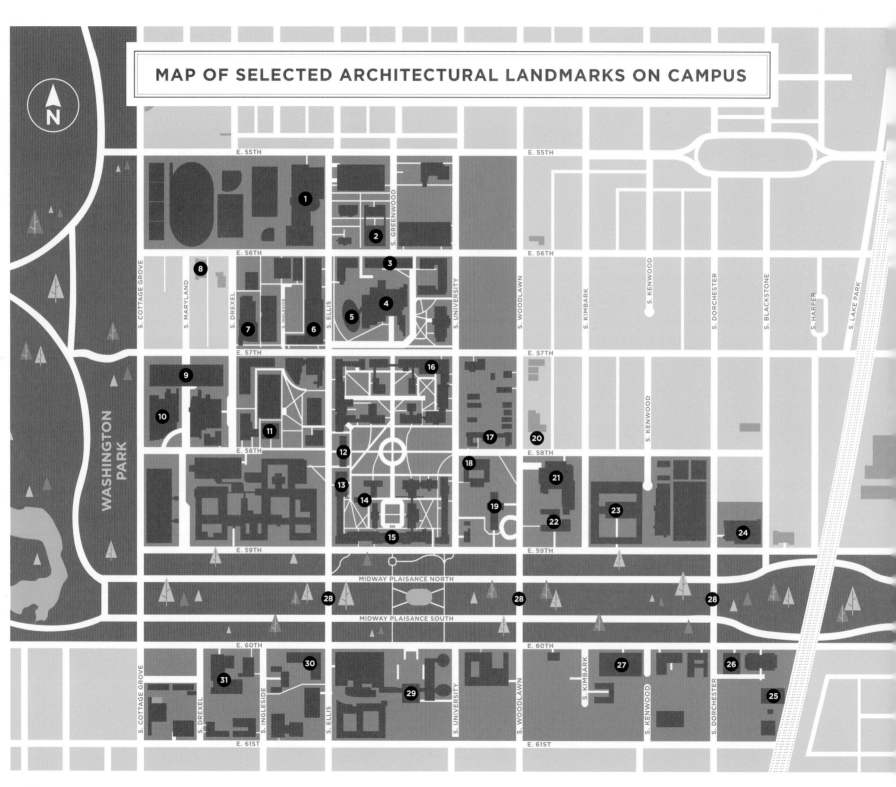

MAP OF SELECTED ARCHITECTURAL LANDMARKS ON CAMPUS

N

WASHINGTON PARK

E. 55TH

E. 56TH

E. 57TH

E. 58TH

E. 59TH

MIDWAY PLAISANCE NORTH

MIDWAY PLAISANCE SOUTH

E. 60TH

E. 61ST

S. COTTAGE GROVE

S. MARYLAND

S. DREXEL

S. INGLESIDE

S. ELLIS

S. GREENWOOD

S. UNIVERSITY

S. WOODLAWN

S. KIMBARK

S. KENWOOD

S. DORCHESTER

S. BLACKSTONE

S. HARPER

S. LAKE PARK

Downtown Chicago,
8 miles north

LAKE MICHIGAN

LAKE SHORE DRIVE

41

MUSEUM OF SCIENCE AND INDUSTRY

S. CORNELL

S. CORNELL

JACKSON PARK

1 Gerald Ratner Athletics Center

2 Smart Museum of Art

3 Max Palevsky Residential Commons

4 Joseph Regenstein Library

5 Joe and Rika Mansueto Library

6 William Eckhardt Research Center

7 Knapp Center for Biomedical Discovery

8 West Campus Combined Utility Plant

9 Center for Care and Discovery

10 Duchossois Center for Advanced Medicine

11 Cummings Life Science Center

12 Administration Building

13 Cobb Hall

14 Bond Chapel

15 William Rainey Harper Memorial Library

16 Tower Group (Mitchell Tower, Hutchinson Commons, Reynolds Club, and Mandel Hall)

17 Hall for Economics

18 Oriental Institute

19 Rockefeller Memorial Chapel

20 Frank Lloyd Wright Robie House

21 Charles M. Harper Center / Booth School of Business

22 Ida Noyes Hall

23 Laboratory Schools

24 International House

25 South Campus Chiller Plant

26 Chicago Theological Seminary

27 New Graduate Residence Hall

28 Midway Crossings

29 Laird Bell Law Quadrangle

30 Reva and David Logan Center for the Arts

31 School of Social Service Administration

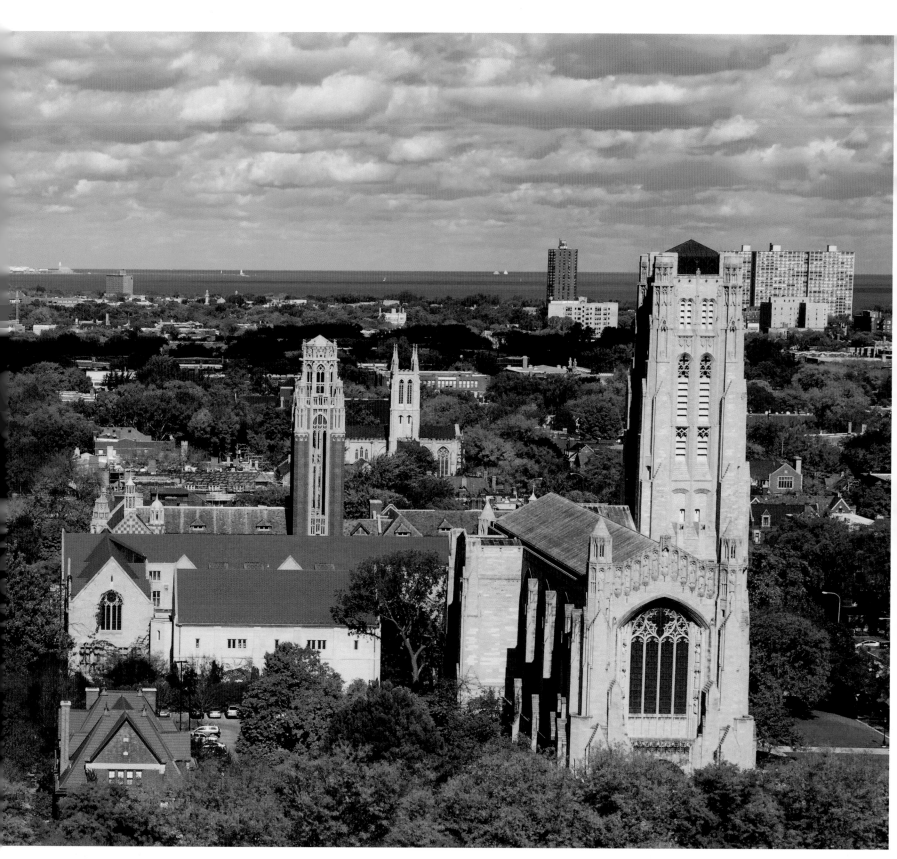

FOREWORD

IN 1895, A FEW YEARS after the University of Chicago was founded, author Robert Herrick wrote: "The university has done more than grow: it has sprung into existence full-armed. And one benefit of this supernatural birth is that its external form has been planned with regard for the *ensemble*."

Such planning for the ensemble began with Henry Ives Cobb's "very latest English Gothic" buildings, which form the heart of the University of Chicago's quadrangles. It continues today as some of the world's finest architects transform traditional English Gothic, with its ties to residential colleges such as Oxford and Cambridge, into an American Gothic flexible enough to meet the needs of a modern research university.

In this volume, Jay Pridmore underscores the tremendous changes that have taken place on the University of Chicago's Hyde Park campus over the past century. Noting architectural detail and institutional history, Jay traces the life story of the campus, from Cobb's original buildings to contemporary additions such as the Joe and Rika Mansueto

THE MAIN QUADRANGLE. A view facing east from the Administration Building.

Library, designed by Helmut Jahn, and the Reva and David Logan Center for the Arts, designed by Tod Williams and Billie Tsien. Yet as much as our campus has changed, we remain stalwart in the belief that the built environment expresses the fundamental character of the university and the evolving ideas that drive the intellectual pursuits here.

The architecture of the University of Chicago inspires, encourages, and supports the pursuit of knowledge in all its forms, sustaining an innovative, creative, and fearless scholarly community whose impact reaches well beyond the university's walls. Three contemporary buildings serve to illustrate this precept.

Mansueto Library is an architectural gem and an engineering marvel. Beneath its ground-level reading room are five stories that hold millions of volumes, each retrievable on demand with the aid of computer-guided robots. Rather than shift collections offsite, with this structure the university affirms the vital role libraries have played in the development of knowledge, the stewardship of history, and the education of generations. Far more than a building, Mansueto represents our belief in libraries, what they meant in the past and what they will mean in the future as they support education and research in new and inventive ways.

The Center for Care and Discovery is the university's newest hospital and the largest building to date on the Hyde Park campus. The center connects patients and families from Chicago and beyond with the university, where they receive state-of-the-art care in a facility designed for present needs and anticipating future ones. Situated next to the Knapp Center for Biomedical Discovery and the Gordon Center for Integrative Science, the Center for Care and Discovery also serves as a magnet, drawing the best minds in medicine to the University of Chicago to forge links between patient care and scholarly activities of research and teaching. Few academic medical centers enjoy such a geographical advantage. This facility represents the university's highest aspirations in understanding and improving the quality of human life.

The new William Eckhardt Research Center, at the corner of Ellis Avenue and 57th Street, is set to open in 2015. This building makes a powerful statement about the nature of scientific research, its design enabling researchers to cross disciplinary boundaries easily. Home to the Institute for Molecular Engineering and some of the university's finest programs in the physical sciences, the building has been designed for structural stability and intense collaboration. It is what university architect Steve Wiesenthal calls a "people collider," with offices interspersed rather than divided by department. As such, it represents the spirit that has guided the University of Chicago since its founding: a spirit of collaboration, interdisciplinarity, community, and discovery.

These three buildings continue the legacy of architecture and ideas at the University of Chicago. That legacy supports the efforts of thousands of people—faculty members, students, alumni, artisans, craftspeople, and many others—who have dedicated themselves to creating an intellectual destination where the power of inquiry guides education and research.

Whether it's the creative expression captured within the Logan Center for the Arts, the architectural echoes of Rockefeller Chapel and Robie House within the design of the Harper Center, the meticulous Arts and Crafts ornamentation of Ida Noyes Hall, the reflection of Oxford in Mitchell Tower, or Eero Saarinen's pleated glass in the Laird Bell Law Quadrangle, every building on this campus is part of the university's story and has a tale of its own to tell.

May this volume provide a fitting introduction to those stories and a fitting welcome to the University of Chicago.

— ROBERT J. ZIMMER

President, The University of Chicago

May 2013

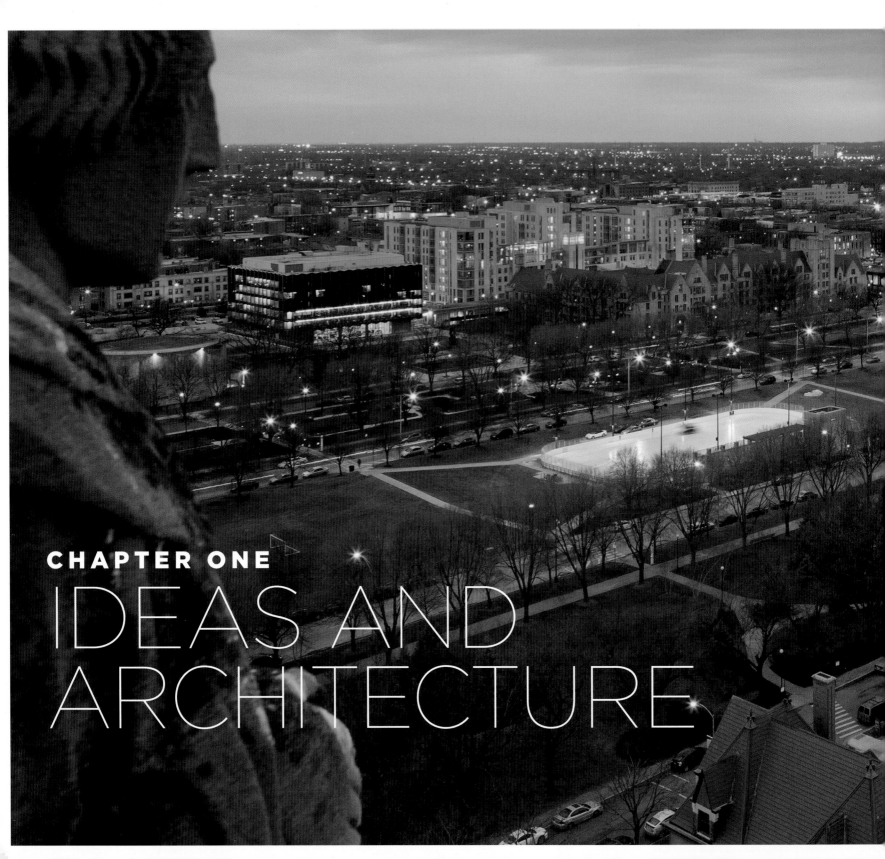

CHAPTER ONE
IDEAS AND ARCHITECTURE

The University of Chicago originated not as a small college as did most universities in the East, but rather with the full-blown ambition of a major university—one that was unique in reflecting from its beginnings the American ideals of openness and accessibility based on merit rather than social position. Just as Chicago is the great American city, so the University of Chicago is the great American university.

— ROBERT J. ZIMMER

THE UNIVERSITY OF CHICAGO'S LEAFY, sprawling campus in Hyde Park is one of the world's great intellectual destinations, and its complexity and diversity are vividly reflected in its architecture. The campus in many respects appears venerable and rich with tradition, and in other ways it seems fresh and mutable as a new idea.

Today, the original quadrangles remain as the founders intended, with gardens surrounded by limestone buildings that feel as ancient as the hills. Yet the courtyards, towers, gates, and gargoyles engage in continuous dialogue with more modern neighbors, the newest among them transparent, seemingly weightless, and gleaming with light. Together the buildings reinforce the university's message that it honors the past even as it gazes into the future.

Architecture has been central to the university's identity since its founding in 1890. By then Chicago had already earned a reputation for innovative architecture. The city's early architects included those collectively known as the Chicago School, famous for

THE SOUTH AND WEST CAMPUS
(chapter opening pages), seen from the tower of Rockefeller Memorial Chapel.

THE MAIN QUADRANGLE
(opposite) in autumn.

THE UNIVERSITY OF CHICAGO provided a backdrop to the eclectic Midway of the 1893 World's Columbian Exposition (*above*). As the university grew, the Midway (*opposite*) became a main axis of the campus.

creating the modern skyscraper. In the shadow of the nascent university, Chicago hosted the 1893 World's Columbian Exposition and created the grandiose White City, America's first major example of City Beautiful urban planning. These and other achievements set high standards for architecture on the University of Chicago campus.

The university has long shown its desire to meet if not exceed those expectations. In the beginning, the founders debated the merits of the chosen site, not just where it was located but how it should be configured. They considered the architectural styles then in vogue—Classical, Romanesque, Gothic. They remained vigilant in guiding the early campus design, and they were generous with their money and their personal engagement. The founders believed that the architecture of Chicago's university should bespeak an institution that exuded ambition and vision.

CHICAGO'S RENAISSANCE SPIRIT

The university's aspirations were fueled by the times. When the institution was founded, the United States was completing its conquest of the frontier, mastering industrialization, and believing fervently in manifest destiny. Chicago, as a new city of immense importance,

served as more than a major hub and staging ground for commerce. It became a symbol of the nation's future. Chicago's wealth outpaced its rapid population growth, and its self-regard often outpaced its wealth. In the early twentieth century, novelist Theodore Dreiser described Chicago as the "Florence of the West . . . a hobo among cities, with the grip of Caesar in its mind." City fathers treated cultural development with the same entrepreneurial drive that they applied to business concerns, and the university benefited from this thoroughgoing spirit.

Like the notion of manifest destiny, Chicago's greatness was considered a self-fulfilling prophecy. Even the Great Chicago Fire became less a setback and more an opportunity to reclaim open spaces. In the fire's wake, the city attracted a wave of architects and builders willing and able to reconceive Chicago. "The flames swept away forever the greater number of monstrous libels on artistic house-building," declared a local publication at the time.

Sensing this as a rare moment, the architects who would make Chicago famous mostly came from elsewhere for the chance to build as no place had been built before. Henry Ives Cobb, William LeBaron Jenney, John Wellborn Root, Louis Sullivan, and Frank Lloyd Wright migrated here looking for ways to engage in new ideas and to realize high ambitions.

Downtown, the Loop prospered as steel-frame structures scraped the sky, dazzling the world with their lofty heights as well as their returns on investment. Surrounding areas prospered too, as railroads collaborated with real estate interests to develop outlying neighborhoods and communities. Indeed, when the university's founders chose Hyde Park, it was a marshy, largely undeveloped southern outpost. But it had rail service and the promise of an active future, so acres of land were drained and reclaimed. To the founders of the university, the less-than-bucolic property around 57th Street represented a slate at least as clean as that provided by the fire.

A CITY'S UNBRIDLED AMBITION

The earliest proponents of the University of Chicago were churchmen who wanted to expand the Baptist Union Theological Seminary. The church organization showed an interest in establishing "a great college, ultimately to be a University, in Chicago," wrote

WASHINGTON PARK LAGOONS provide a pastoral counterpoint to the University of Chicago Medical Campus.

COBB HALL, Henry Ives Cobb, 1892. The university's first building (named not for the architect but for the donor) established the campus style for the next fifty years.

JOHN D. ROCKEFELLER   WILLIAM RAINEY HARPER

THE HALL FOR ECONOMICS' future home, renovation, Ann Beha Architects, expected completion 2014. This Herbert Riddle building (1928) once housed the Seminary Co-op Bookstore in its basement.

Frederick T. Gates, a high-ranking Baptist clergyman from Minneapolis. "Between the Allegheny and the Rocky Mountains there is not to be found another city in which such an institution as we need could . . . achieve wide influence or retain supremacy among us."

The idea attracted the attention of another Baptist: John D. Rockefeller, a man who knew something of big plans. Rockefeller required some convincing, but ultimately he pledged $600,000, an amount that would swell over time to $37 million. A wealth of correspondence ensued, debating what kind of an institution there should be and how it might address the problems of the growing metropolis, become a laboratory for research across disciplines, and bring the uplifting influence of a large university to a city that did not have one within its limits.

Rockefeller's interest, indeed his strength, lay in the realm of brick and mortar, and he exhorted the founders not to think small. "Do not on account of scarcity of money fail to do the right thing in constructing new buildings," he wrote to Thomas Goodspeed, a trustee and secretary to the board. "We must in some way secure sufficient funds to make it what it ought to be."

Local collaborators shared Rockefeller's interest in a new university. Many were non-Baptists from families whose viewpoints were shaped by the risk and drama of acquiring significant wealth in a new city. Charles Hutchinson, a banker and trader, was illustrative. He left a successful career in business to concentrate on building cultural institutions in Chicago. Hutchinson assumed a pivotal role in the creation of the University of Chicago and, along with his friend, steel magnate Martin Ryerson, persuaded the newly recruited board to acquire a four-block site.

Another key player in the conception of the University of Chicago was William Rainey Harper, who came to the Midwest from Yale. He shared the high aspirations of Chicagoans to create an original, fundamentally new enterprise. Harper envisioned a college, graduate schools, an extension division, and publishing house that would grow under the same umbrella. He insisted that it be a university (not a mere "college") of diverse parts, unified by the spirit of inquiry, of Socratic debate, of shared purpose and outsized ambition. He and the other founders were convinced that the university was an essential engine of the city's social and intellectual advancement.

HENRY IVES COBB'S CHICAGO GOTHIC

For the physical plan and architectural design, the founding trustees considered six local firms. Chicago's architectural talent was adept at executing large projects, maintaining budgets, and creating designs that consistently impressed (albeit grudgingly) the critics from the East Coast. Chicago School architects designed for a demanding city: for developers who craved square footage, for building occupants who loved abundant natural light and fresh air, and for Chicagoans who aspired to distinctive and occasionally sublime architecture. The trustees appeared determined to create a campus as emblematic of the university mission as the downtown skyscrapers were of the city's soaring economic ambitions.

The winning proposal was submitted by Henry Ives Cobb, whose portfolio in Chicago included tall office buildings along with well-appointed residences. Cobb's was not the most beautifully rendered entry, but the relationship he had formed with Hutchinson and Ryerson—Hutchinson was a member of the Chicago Athletic Association, which Cobb had recently designed to significant praise—may have helped him secure the university commission.

Cobb's original proposal for buildings in the Romanesque style was quickly revised to the Gothic, which lent the campus an air of distinction and erudition—this in a city that had often defended itself against an image as hog butcher. Not long after the first buildings went up, the magazine and arbiter *Architectural Record* endorsed the university's campus in conception as well as execution. The Gothic style was "selected as far as possible to remind one of the old English Universities of Cambridge and Oxford; in fact to remove the mind of the student from the busy mercantile conditions of Chicago."

The choice of Gothic offered other advantages as well. Among them was the timeless quality of the buildings, which "struck Gothic notes of permanence and immortality," as Harper and his compatriots desired. The style harkened to medieval times, a period romanticized as the antithesis of industrialization, impersonalization, and the oppression of the working classes. That bygone age of chivalry, noted for artisanship and individuality, had inspired writers such as Walter Scott, John Ruskin, and William Morris to revive

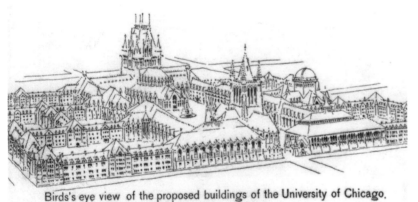

HENRY IVES
COBB

HENRY IVES COBB'S ORIGINAL SCHEME
for the campus, 1893. The plans included a
chapel and library on the quads.

Birds's eye view of the proposed buildings of the University of Chicago.
From the approved plans.

medieval customs, including architecture. On a practical level, Gothic's asymmetrical massing enabled numerous building types—libraries, classrooms, and laboratories among them. The style's endless variations of detail assured that the campus would remain unified even as it grew over time.

EMBRACE OF SUITABLE TRADITIONS

There were dissenters, naturally, who found the style distasteful, but they did not number among the trustees or others who could block the decision. Thorstein Veblen, the eminent sociologist, saw the campus where he worked as out-of-date, and derided "the disjointed grotesqueries of an eclectic and modified Gothic." He believed that it would end up a regrettable choice when the style fell out of fashion.

Frank Lloyd Wright was also dismayed by the theatricality of the Gothic style, modern 500 years earlier, for an institution that aimed to offer the most up-to-date learning in many fields. In 1930 he wondered aloud why "an American University in a land of Democratic ideals in a Machine Age [should] be characterized by second-hand adaptation of Gothic forms."

Veblen's denunciation is easy to dismiss, for he was a social scientist, not an architect or designer. But Wright's critique is not discounted so readily. He himself had been influenced by Gothic architecture, which, like the prairie style, was grounded in organic and natural forms. Indeed, Wright possessed a genius for geometric harmonies and asymmetric massing, features that also made Gothic a durable and influential style.

It is intriguing to imagine the University of Chicago as designed by Frank Lloyd Wright. His famous Robie House, on the edge of campus, might seem an implausible template to line the quadrangles; a more likely one may be Hitchcock Hall, which was built on the quads in 1902. Hitchcock is Dwight Perkins's blend of Wright-inspired organic design and Gothic revival. It features unique floral ornamentation, inspired by Wright's mentor Louis Sullivan, and a prairie-style-like floor plan more intricate, even labyrinthine, than that of most Gothic revival buildings on campus.

But as far as Wright is concerned, he would have been much too cranky to design in the collective environment of a university. Cobb, in contrast, was a brilliant collaborator. As for the suitability of Cobb's influence in the ten years and sixteen buildings of his tenure

for the university, we can defer to no less an arbiter than Eero Saarinen, who took on master planning for the university around the time he designed the Law School, completed in 1959. He observed that the university's Gothic style was used not just by Cobb but by a succession of later architects for almost forty years. Saarinen judged the result "a beautiful, harmonious visual picture" and implied that early choices, not just of the Gothic styling but of uniform materials (Indiana limestone) and thoughtful proportions, inspired later architects to build agreeable neighbors.

As we'll see, the design decisions that informed the university's architecture were prescient and influential. Their long-standing emphasis on public space, both as a planning motif and to encourage intellectual collaboration, has been manifest in new science quadrangles, in the winter garden of the Booth School of Business's Charles M. Harper Center, and in other places that encourage interaction. In many ways, innovative buildings on campus heed the university's vivid past as much as they reach toward its future.

The university's Gothic revival may have had its heyday in the early twentieth century, but it has been influential well beyond that period. Other styles have also left their own stamp on the Hyde Park campus as it has expanded with the times. Many so-called modern buildings may even appear at odds with the carved towers and turrets of old. But in them we detect an architectural tradition—and a consistent eye for interpreting it— that runs deeper than styles or superficial appearance.

Today we see contemporary buildings through a lens colored by history. In new architecture, like the old, the best buildings deftly incorporate the site, scale, and spirit of the institution. The long-term beauty and suitability of any single building on campus reflect not only the skill of the architect but the character of nearby buildings as well— structures that harmoniously define and affirm the university's identity.

ROBIE HOUSE, Frank Lloyd Wright, 1909.
This building is recognized as an icon of American architecture.

ROBIE HOUSE assumes a leading role in Blue Balliett's book *The Wright 3*, which evokes a visual symphony of architectural detail and play of light.

To view a video of Blue Balliett discussing Robie House, scan the QR code at left and select "Robie House."

The Robie House Symphony

CHILDREN'S BOOK AUTHOR BLUE BALLIETT and her family live within walking distance of Robie House, Frank Lloyd Wright's prairie style masterpiece in Hyde Park. Of her fascination with the house, Balliett has said, "I love the idea of something made of brick or stone or wood, something that is not supposed to be alive, communicating. . . . Although, of course, that's impossible . . . or is it?"

In *The Wright 3,* Balliett draws from the history of Robie House, imagining that it is once again under threat of demolition. A group of sixth graders decides to try to save it, and the students learn to appreciate the house not only as architecture but as a work of art. Mrs. Sharpe, a former occupant, describes the features of the house that bring it to life:

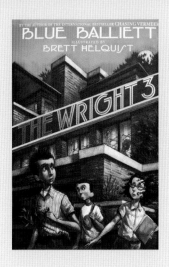

Living in that house felt a bit like living in a slowly turning kaleidoscope. The light captured by those windows changes by the hour, and sometimes even by the second, and yet what you see always fits perfectly with everything else. It's almost as if Wright managed to set up a resonance between the structure itself and all of the details—art glass, ceiling grilles, rugs, lamps, balconies—that changes continuously and yet remains seamless. I'm not sure anyone has ever been able to figure out exactly how he did it. A symphony, that's what the place is like—a complex Bach symphony that sharpens your mind even if you can't comprehend every strand of harmony. And when you stand inside, it's almost as if you become part of the art yourself, an instrument in Mr. Wright's hands. There's the feeling of belonging to someone else's imagination.

CHAPTER TWO

THE GOTHIC CAMPUS

THE TRUSTEES OF THE NEW and as-yet-unformed University of Chicago were in a hurry. In April 1891, they invited six architectural offices to submit proposals to build on the four-block site assembled just a few months before. Among the competitors was Adler and Sullivan, the best-known firm in Chicago at the time. Within weeks the trustees chose Henry Ives Cobb, architect of Loop skyscrapers, country houses, and a few years later the Newberry Library. By early June, the trustees most involved in building concerns, Charles Hutchinson and Martin Ryerson, visited Cobb's studio to discuss the drawings he had submitted.

Like the other architects vying for the commission, Cobb had proposed buildings in the then-fashionable Romanesque manner, the style made popular by the prominent Boston architect Henry Hobson Richardson. Richardson's rusticated walls and heavy arches were admired throughout the country for their strength and frank expression of underlying structure—and by extension their American character. Yet, once settled

HULL GATE (*pages 16–17*) leading to the courtyard of Hull Biological Laboratories, Henry Ives Cobb, 1897.

COBB'S ORIGINAL LAYOUT (*opposite*) featured a quadrangle system, which created intimate courtyards and long vistas through its network of interlocking outdoor spaces.

WIEBOLDT HALL, Coolidge and Hodgdon, 1928.

in Cobb's office, the trustees expressed doubts about the architect's initial scheme for sprawling, fortresslike buildings. They wondered whether they might take the architecture in another direction.

If given an "absolutely independent choice," they asked, what style would Cobb select for the campus? "The very latest English Gothic," Cobb replied, referring to the architecture inspired by Oxford and Cambridge and recently adopted by Yale and Trinity in New England. The swiftness with which they agreed to Cobb's preference indicated that beyond his skill in design or draftsmanship, Cobb's skills as a collaborator suited him well for the university project.

This is not to downplay Cobb's credentials, which were well established before the University of Chicago commission. He was already known to Hutchinson for his work on the Chicago Athletic Association's building, whose blend of skyscraper construction and athletic-club interior was intended to make it "outrival the East," as the *Tribune* wrote when the structure was going up. Cobb had also designed Lake Geneva homes for leading Chicago families, among whom the founders of the university numbered.

It must have been clear to both the architect and the trustees that they shared important values. Cobb came from the Brahmin social class in Boston, and he was a man with whom affluent Chicagoans like Hutchinson and Ryerson could feel comfortable. At the same time, Cobb had moved to Chicago for its energy and willingness to eclipse hidebound traditions. He was attracted to the kind of client who was building not just growing businesses but ambitious institutions—a "cultural entrepreneur," in the words of Cobb's biographer, Edward Wolner. As an architect, Cobb reconciled the opposing forces of innovation and tradition. He could design for simple construction and noble imagery.

THE GOTHIC TEMPLATE

The decision to adopt the Gothic style carried the same intuitive charge as so much of Chicago's swift development. While considered too ornamental for the Chicago School, the Gothic template had long been lauded by critics like John Ruskin as symbols of truth and timelessness. As a practical matter, Gothic's endless variations, drawn from its long history, enabled a unified yet differentiated assembly of buildings.

COBB GATE (*opposite*), Henry Ives Cobb, 1900. The Gothic style inspired varied entries to the quadrangles and symbolic figures carved in stone. Wieboldt features the portraits of classic authors in what was once the Department of Modern Languages.

A month after meeting with Hutchinson and Ryerson, Cobb submitted an elaborate sketch of the Gothic revival campus as he envisioned it. The drawing is fanciful, especially in scale, with its two largest buildings—a chapel and library—featuring unlikely towers of fourteen or more stories. Yet the basics of the Gothic style are clear. Quadrangles, inspired by medieval cloisters, appear rarefied and protected from the hurly-burly of the city. The variety of building types suited the many functions envisioned for the university. The scheme had classrooms and dormitories, which, along with the library and chapel, would eventually fill an elegant, distinctive campus.

COBB HALL (named after Silas B. Cobb). A view from the C-Bench, where tradition once dictated that only privileged students (seniors, lettermen, and their companions) could sit.

As the first buildings were going up, conversations focused not on questions of style but on the slowness of Cobb's work. To handle the university and his other projects, the architect had increased his staff to one hundred thirty people, but the founders became impatient as Cobb continued to work at his own stubborn pace. "We have haunted his office," wrote Thomas Goodspeed, secretary to the board, to Harper. "We have urged, exhorted, entreated." Nothing worked—though, as we'll see, Cobb's stubbornness was vindicated.

Architectural challenges did not constrain the university project in other important respects. Early in 1892, Chicagoan Silas B. Cobb (no relation to the architect) pledged $150,000 for classrooms, offices, and other functions, for which his name would grace the university's first building. "There is no more important public enterprise than the University of Chicago," the donor wrote.

As ground had been broken and the donation was in hand, architect Cobb finally produced working drawings. Cobb Hall opened in the fall of 1892, the only campus building to greet the first five hundred ten students enrolled in undergraduate, graduate, and divinity schools. Among its many assets, Cobb Hall's picturesque design set a worthy standard for the sixteen buildings that architect Cobb would create in the decade to come. Necessarily, the first building served as a multi-use structure, housing a chapel on the first floor, some sixty rooms for academic departments, plus the president's office. Goodspeed praised

the building: "It has a record for general utility which no other University building can ever have," he wrote. Cobb Hall used construction technologies developed for city office buildings: masonry bearing walls around the perimeter and iron supports within. This enabled the moving of interior walls when needs changed, as they certainly would.

The exterior looked and functioned equally well. Cobb used the conventions of Tudor Gothic to design a fundamentally simple building. Its massing remained straightforward, almost boxlike save for the projecting and receding walls. Ornamental details caressed the eye at certain points, especially in the towers and around the central entry. Above the doors, a Tudor-arch window drew attention away from the otherwise plain profile and fenestration of much of the rest of the building.

In subtle ways, Cobb Hall was built for a campus that was a work in progress. When the building sat largely alone (Gates-Blake and Goodspeed dorms soon went up on the side), its stately symmetry reflected its role as the seat of the new university. As the campus filled out and nearby buildings went up, Cobb Hall gained the asymmetry typical of the

KENT CHEMICAL LABORATORY, Henry Ives Cobb, 1894. Kent remains one of Cobb's finest works for its distinctive massing, which includes an octagonal lecture hall with intricate crockets and cornices.

Gothic style: the frontal view from the quad was essentially split, with half forming a corner of the central quadrangle and the other half delineating the adjacent corner of the quadrangle just south. This mutability points not only to Cobb's mastery of Gothic forms but also to his understanding that the campus would evolve and change as time passed.

With Cobb Hall and subsequent buildings—Kent Chemical Laboratory, Ryerson Physical Laboratory, Walker Museum, and Haskell Hall—one began to see an otherworldly place of carved Indiana limestone, a material plentiful enough to be used on

campus for more than a century. Cobb had also demonstrated that Gothic architecture offered form-follows-function modernity. We see it in Kent, with its large octagonal lecture hall, unlike any other Gothic form but harmonious nonetheless. We see it in the original skylights of Haskell, which invited natural light into exhibit spaces. To the casual eye, these features blend nicely with the medieval passageways, crenellated towers, and gargoyles and grotesques. But Cobb's template highlighted modern adaptations of the Gothic—even an observatory atop Ryerson—asserting that the campus was functional, not simply a stage set.

THE REFINED OXONIAN

In 1900, Charles Hutchinson visited Europe with Charles Coolidge, partner of the prominent Boston architectural firm Shepley, Rutan and Coolidge. As successor to the preeminent firm owned by Henry Hobson Richardson, Coolidge's office enjoyed great prestige and won commissions for iconic buildings all over the country. Hutchinson had already worked with Coolidge on the Art Institute of Chicago. Now friends, the two spent time in Oxford, discussing designs for new buildings at the University of Chicago.

Among other objectives, Hutchinson wanted Coolidge to design a commons hall that would bear Hutchinson's name. Predictably, and perhaps unfairly, the trustees took this opportunity to replace Cobb as the university architect with Coolidge's firm. Even before he and Hutchinson left England, Coolidge had workmen take detailed measurements of Christ Church Hall, built in the 1500s at Oxford, which has also served as a model for distinctive features of other universities, notably Cornell and the National University of Ireland.

Hutchinson, by this time president of the board, wrote excitedly to Harper, "I am coming home with great ideas of what our future buildings should be, and only wish that we might begin all over again." By now, the university had more money and could aspire to more elaborate buildings. One senses that the longer the trustees were involved in building, the more they believed they could replicate the great, ageless universities of Europe.

The Tower Group, a cluster of buildings around the northeast edge of the quads, differed from Cobb's more practical buildings. The Coolidge concept began with the faithful reproduction of historical elements. Hutchinson Commons incorporates much of

HUTCHINSON COMMONS (*opposite*) and **MITCHELL TOWER** (*right*), Shepley, Rutan and Coolidge, 1903. Both reflect a turn away from Cobb's utilitarian Chicago Gothic toward Charles Coolidge's Oxonian archetypes. Hutchinson resembles Oxford's Christ Church Hall, and Mitchell Tower is a simplified version of the tower at Magdalen College.

the massing and detail of the Christ Church prototype. It also adds aisles to either side for a kitchen and café, gestures that demonstrate not just the skill of the architect but also the adaptability of the Gothic style. Next to the commons, Mitchell Tower represents a version of the tower at Magdalen College, Oxford, completed in 1509. Adjacent to those is the Reynolds Club, in the image of another Oxford model, St. John's College, built in the 1400s.

Then there was the introduction of carved iconography and the gargoyles, both of which proliferated under Coolidge. It was hardly outlandish for the trustees to seek symbolic buildings or to fill them with statues, reliefs, and other imagery. As Gothic architecture, initially cathedrals, represented the metaphorical universe, their builders elaborated them with figures and epigrams. In like manner, the university seal was designed in 1912 by a Boston artist who often worked for Shepley, Rutan and Coolidge, and it was later elaborated in brass for the entry between Hutchinson and Reynolds.

In many other buildings as well, the Gothic idiom inspired volumes of personal expression in gargoyles and grotesques. Rarely did the architects (and the people directing them) miss a teaching moment. Along the cornice on the Classics Building are the figures of Horace and Cicero, among others. Carved into the exterior of Rosenwald Hall are Leonardo da Vinci and Marco Polo, who made early discoveries in geology and geography, subjects originally taught within.

The William Rainey Harper Memorial Library took the idea of iconography a step
further, with more elaborate narratives suggested outside and in. Harper's towers were
similar to each other in dimension but vastly different in profile. The intentional difference
was clearly a nod to Gothic asymmetry. But on the notion that nothing at the University of
Chicago goes without discursive explanation, a theory evolved that the west tower, which
resembles one at Kings College, Cambridge, has battlements that symbolize the secular
state. The east tower, after a design at Christ Church, has Byzantine imagery that appears
ecclesiastical. According to local lore, this signifies the separation of church and state.
Alternatively it might suggest their unity and the University of Chicago's origins in both
the divine and secular realms. In any case, the nature of the Gothic invites varied and often
elaborate interpretations.

ARCHITECTURE OF MORAL UPLIFT

Chicago's "late Gothic" also gave unprecedented attention to interiors. In Harper Library,
the awe of the vaulted reading room space in the Arley D. Cathy Learning Center is
enhanced by abundant symbology, printer's marks, and coats of arms, suggesting the depth

IDA NOYES HALL (*right and opposite*), Shepley, Rutan and Coolidge, 1916. Ida Noyes Hall, named after the late wife of donor LaVerne Noyes, was built to house university women who neither dined with nor engaged in athletic activities with men. Rich in architectural detail, it features an elaborate cloister and finely wrought interior.

BARTLETT GYMNASIUM (*pages 32–33*), Shepley, Rutan and Coolidge, 1904. Now Bartlett Dining Commons, Bartlett Gym was the first permanent gymnasium on campus. The mural of a medieval tournament was painted by the donor's son Frederick Clay Bartlett.

IDA NOYES   LAVERNE NOYES

of tradition therein. Other buildings extend the Gothic idea in even more marked ways. Bartlett Gymnasium boasts a magnificent mural depicting chivalrous athletic contests. It was painted by Frederick Clay Bartlett, son of the building's donor (who gave it to honor another, deceased, son). Also significant is the clear span space of the former basketball court, now a dining hall, which was constructed of beamwork not particularly Gothic but an example of form and function that recalls the great vaulted cathedrals of Europe.

Elsewhere on campus, a more refined Arts and Crafts approach brought new lavishness to a building of particular significance. Ida Noyes Hall was created as a commons for women, who had been barred from places like the Reynolds Club and Bartlett Gymnasium for reasons considered proper even at a coeducational institution. In 1915 LaVerne Noyes, who had made his fortune in farm implements, donated funds for the construction of a building to honor his late wife, Ida. It would be a place for women to dine and swim; it would also inculcate "tolerance, sympathy, kindness, the generous word and the helpful act," said women's dean Marion Talbot.

SCIENTIA

nt of
ucation

ly Sports
dedicated
ry of
Bartlett
00

How happy is he born and taught that serveth not anoth

At Ida Noyes Hall's dedication, President Harry Pratt Judson was apparently disturbed by the splendor and presumed expense of the interiors, which had oak wainscoting, gessoed ceilings, and a stair rail with grapes and vines in hand-wrought iron. Professor Edith Foster Flint bid the president relax, saying that "we agreed that its beauty ought to be educative." She added that the building itself had inspired more students to read Ruskin's writing on the moral uplift of the Gothic. "[T]he campus buildings in general and Ida Noyes Hall in particular had whetted their appetite for such knowledge," she said.

SEEKING A "MODERN" GOTHIC

In succeeding decades, the Great Depression—and the movement toward simpler and more modern design—signaled the end of the university's indulgence in ornate dreams in stone. Moreover, the aging of a generation of talented, anonymous craftsmen—iron workers, sculptors and stone masons, and woodworkers, many trained in the Old World—necessarily rendered buildings such as Rosenwald and Ida Noyes a thing of the past.

In this and other ways, the building of Rockefeller Memorial Chapel in 1928, though Gothic in profile, was visible proof that the campus was in a state of evolution. Bond Chapel, constructed just two years earlier in the southwest quad, retained a traditional cast even with its Sullivanesque and more modern ornamentation, which at its best brought the inanimate materials of stone and metal to life.

Rockefeller, in contrast, was larger, monumental, and simpler—a sign of the university's expansion out from the original seven quads to face the Midway. But the Gothic spirit still applied. To design the chapel, the trustees engaged Bertram Grosvenor Goodhue of New York, one of the country's leading architects. Goodhue, along with ex-partner Ralph Adams Cram, was a famous proponent of the Gothic revival and designer of prominent churches around the country. What the trustees may not have realized was that Goodhue had been deeply influenced by the modern tendency to simplify with less ornament than had been customary, especially for churches. When Goodhue presented his initial scheme for the chapel, President Ernest DeWitt Burton complained that it seemed less decorative than the university expected. Perhaps contradictorily, he also voiced concerns about the budget.

Goodhue died in 1924. Burton died the following year, before the chapel went up. By then, fortunately, they had agreed on a design that Burton believed resembled

ROCKEFELLER MEMORIAL CHAPEL, Bertram Grosvenor Goodhue, 1928. Its smooth walls and less elaborate ornamentation reflect a more modern Gothic style, setting off the vaulted interior and directing the eye toward structural details.

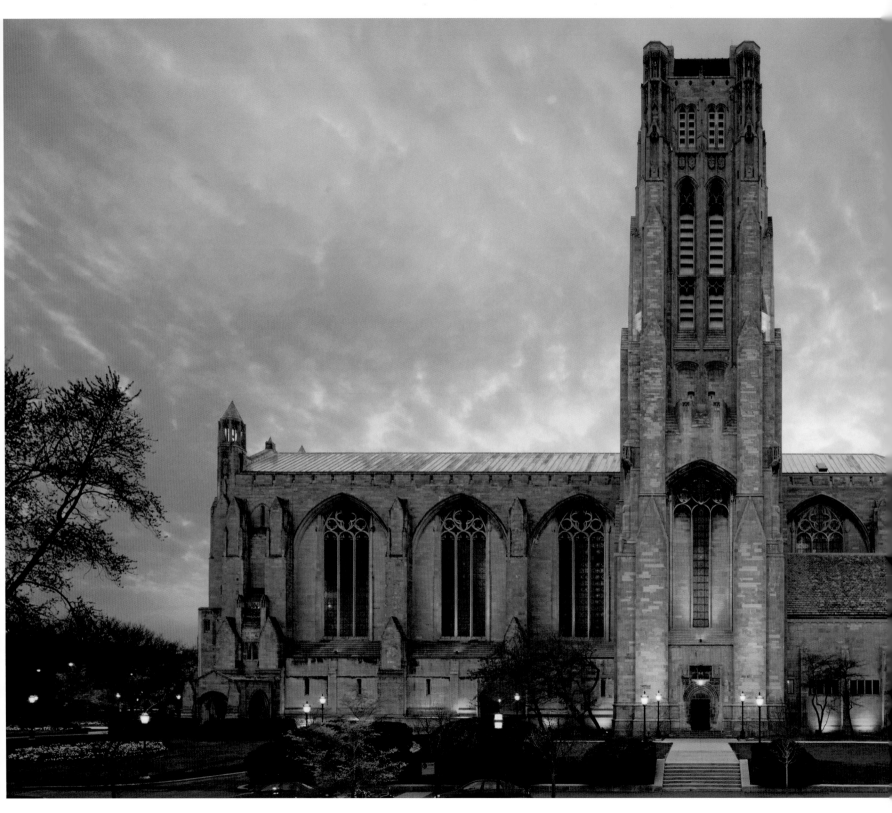

Liverpool Cathedral, a model of modern Gothic revival. Now the university chapel met budgetary constraints in part because elaborate carving, otherwise ubiquitous on religious structures, was replaced by flat surfaces.

As Rockefeller Chapel's massing was a sign of the modern world advancing, so was the detail and, particularly, the ecumenicism of the iconography that it did exhibit. Niches pierce the roofline of the facade, with figures ranging from St. Francis of Assisi to Zoroaster. Their identities are not apparent from the ground, but the tableau enlivens the exterior. It also inspires discourse among members of the community, who over the years have been drawn to theological complexity just as they have been to striking architecture.

Despite its touches of modernity, the chapel seems timeless, entirely at one with the rest of the Gothic campus. Goodhue's objective in architecture, far from reproducing historic models, was to create a style "malleable enough to be molded to the designer's will, as readily toward the calm perfection of the Parthenon as toward the majesty and restless mystery of Chartres."

The founders of the university could not have expressed their objective more eloquently. Critics over the years have parsed the university's Gothic revival buildings, deeming Coolidge better than Henry Ives Cobb or Swift Hall more "modern" than Harold Leonard Stuart Hall, but such distinctions have been obscured by time. More important is the straddling of calm introspection and restless mystery that Cobb achieved in his initial efforts. The architecture of the university has been judged by that standard ever since, long after plates of glass replaced sections of limestone and modern cable supports held buildings aloft where flying buttresses might once have soared.

ROCKEFELLER CHAPEL, while ecclesiastical in aspect, was meant to serve all faiths, including "happy agnostics," in the words of one chaplain.

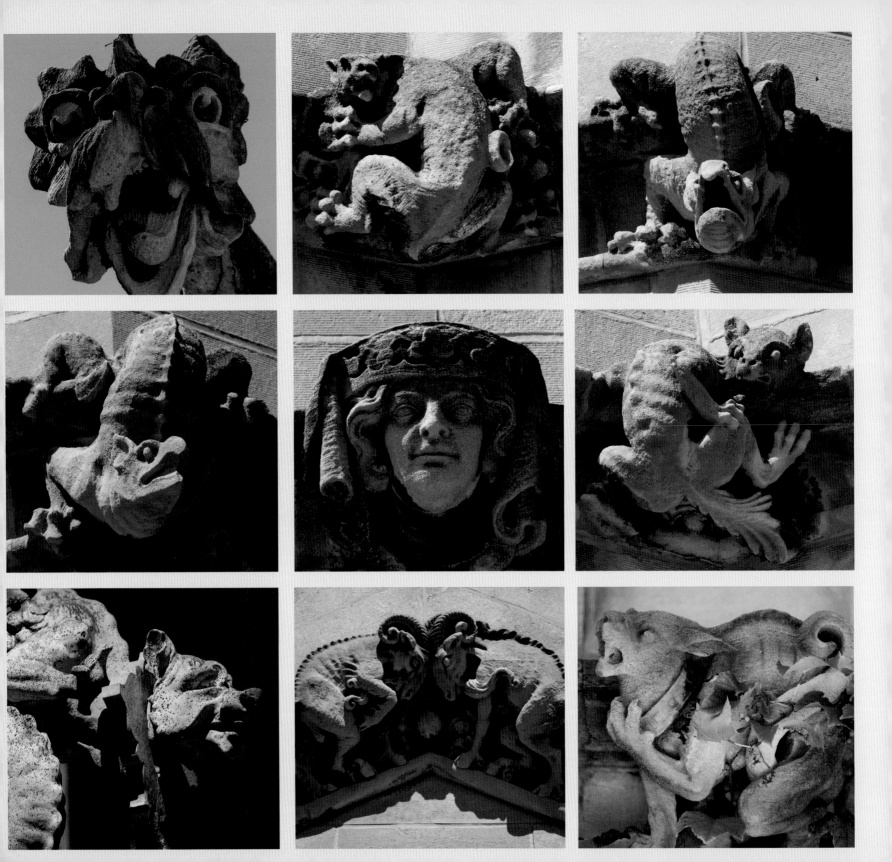

SUBVERSIVE CARICATURE is not the point of the seven hundred or so gargoyles, chimeras, and grotesques that adorn the Gothic revival buildings of the University of Chicago. But it was characteristic of their medieval models, the functional ornaments of Gothic architecture carved into fantastic beasts that represent, to some, the stuff of nightmares.

A gargoyle is an ornamental down spout or drain pipe, the word deriving from the French *le gorge,* for throat. In common parlance it has come to signify nearly any figurative ornament on the exterior of a building, though such decoration that does not include the down spout function is more properly termed a grotesque or chimera.

Gargoyles and Grotesques

The chimeric figures of Cobb Gate, donated by Henry Ives Cobb near the end of his tenure as university architect, carry special meaning for undergraduates. Legend has it that the snarling figures on the corners represent admissions officers; the clawing figures ascending are first-, second-, and third-year students; and at the top is a triumphant fourth-year.

As buildings were planned, a faculty committee on symbolism was formed to govern what type of ornamentation would be used, and architectural decoration increasingly included sculpted elements that depicted the activity taking place within the structures. Thus Bond Chapel bears biblical iconography. The Classics Building is embellished with the heads of Cicero, Seneca, and other philosophers. And Rosenwald Hall, originally built to house the geography and geology departments, features working geologists and their motto, "Dig and discover." Stone carvings reflected not just a building's function but its time as well; the Social Science Research Building is decorated with a relief of an adding machine.

And so, writes Jean Block in her history of campus architecture, *The Uses of Gothic,* traditional Gothic embellishment gains modernistic symbols and in many ways leaves Gothic behind.

THESE FIGURES, whether carved in stone or cast in bronze, are sometimes historical and other times drawn entirely from the architect's (or even craftsman's) imagination. They continue to fuel discussion, debate, and urban legends.

CHAPTER THREE

THE OLMSTED EFFECT

Its civilizing and humanizing influence is something wholly incalculable.
The visitors belong to every class and grade of society, yet every one seems there
to be on his good behaviour.

— ANDREAS SIMON,
on Washington Park, adjacent to campus

FEW CAMPUS MASTER PLANS have influenced as many architects over such a long period as the original design for the University of Chicago. The strength of the plan lies largely in seven interlocking quadrangles, as laid out by architect Henry Ives Cobb in 1891, and in the Gothic revival style that Cobb established in his early buildings. Yet one critical decision for building the university was made before Cobb ever arrived on the scene. That was the acquisition of the site, a process that began when Marshall Field donated a three-block strip from 56th to 59th Streets. The trustees were pleased by the donation. Hyde Park and Field's land would work for the new university.

But that did not end the matter. The trustees considered the long, narrow parcel to be imperfect. So they negotiated with Field to trade one of the donated blocks, purchase another, and assemble a four-block square. The parcel now constituted "the ideal site," wrote Thomas Goodspeed in his early history of the university. Besides the sufficiency of its size, there were the benefits of its shape, which made it commodious in every direction.

THE MAIN QUADRANGLE (*pages 40–41*)

THIS VIEW (*opposite*) of the university, from the Ferris Wheel of the 1893 World's Columbian Exposition, reveals the beginnings of the campus lines, both formal and naturalized.

Though not obvious in the sandy soil and shallow marshes of the unbuilt twenty-three acres, it became the perfect blank slate for Cobb's scheme of Gothic structures and outdoor spaces.

Cobb's plan drew deeply from history. But it also accommodated the future so well that architects commissioned for new campus buildings still reference the courtyards, gates, and towers as they design thoroughly contemporary structures. The original plan cloistered its learned precincts from the outside world, metaphorically protecting the university's high calling from the harsher realities of urban life. Yet the outdoor spaces also flowed, parklike and panoramic, into the surrounding neighborhoods. It represented the synthesis of opposites, the intimate and the grand, separate yet connected to the outside world. Even more than the famous carved limestone of its buildings, the early carving of space became key to the campus's long-term development.

Carefully proportioned quadrangles "helped transform a suburban idyll into an integral part of a modern city," wrote Cobb's biographer, Edward Wolner. The university's influence on Hyde Park represented an ongoing if unstated objective of the trustees and of Field, who still owned significant property in the area. Within a few years, well-heeled homeowners—many of them faculty members—bought lots, built houses, and created a community inextricable from the university.

A CITY IN THE GARDEN

Hyde Park, which was annexed to the city in 1889, had been created more than three decades before by real estate entrepreneur Paul Cornell, whose interest was residential development. He purchased three hundred acres seven miles south of the Loop, then traded sixty of those acres as right-of-way to the Illinois Central Railroad in exchange for promised commuter service. Growth was initially slow, but cool breezes off the lake eventually attracted affluent residents as marshland was reclaimed. Cornell and local power brokers exhibited their farsightedness, meanwhile, by setting aside open space for parks, which became models of urban planning.

THE QUADRANGLES of Cobb's layout have multiplied and grown verdant under the Olmsted Brothers' landscape design.

Enlightened attitudes also led to the hiring of Frederick Law Olmsted and Calvert Vaux to design landscapes for what became Washington and Jackson Parks and the Midway Plaisance. The firm of Olmsted and Vaux was already famous for creating meadows, woods, and waterways on urban landscapes, most famously New York's Central Park. The Chicago project began in 1870, a year before the fire, and was finally completed when Olmsted returned to landscape the 1893 World's Columbian Exposition. Rowboats on ponds and open air concerts were among the "civilizing and humanizing" elements of Olmsted's parks. They also helped make Hyde Park desirable.

The university on the edge of the Midway was no less idealistic a project. The trustees were determined to influence the entire city, and even American democracy, with this new institution of higher education. But they were hard-headed enough to know that the idea would grow only if Chicago and its economy prospered along with the human spirit. This meant attracting business. If the founders' keen interest in subdividing Hyde Park real estate appeared at odds with their high-minded ideals for the university, the site they chose was well suited to mediate between the apparent antitheses. Undeniably, the university's position on the edge of both the urban grid and bucolic garden aligned with Chicago's aspirations as expressed in its motto *Urbs in Horto*.

A SLOWLY EMBROIDERED LANDSCAPE

In the beginning, the campus landscape did not look like much of anything. The lawns were a construction site and scrub oaks did little to improve matters, and there things stood for a decade. By 1899, the trustees yearned to realize the campus's potential beauty, so they hired O. C. Simonds, a landscape architect with a national reputation (Frederick Law Olmsted at that point was elderly and frail). Simonds proposed a landscape in the romantic vein, with winding paths and a gentle roll. But neither the trustees nor the faculty liked his design.

"It was more like Graceland Cemetery [which Simonds had designed a few years before] than a college campus," observes Richard Bumstead, the university's current landscape architect. So the trustees sought another approach. In 1902 they engaged the firm of Olmsted Brothers (sons of Frederick Law), who had worked with the university's new architects, Shepley, Rutan and Coolidge, at Stanford. John C. Olmsted agreed

WALKER MUSEUM, Henry Ives Cobb, 1893. Redbud and sugar maple trees color the landscape near this building, originally a natural history museum.

(perhaps self-servingly) that Simonds's plan was too dramatic. The quadrangles' landscape, he believed, should be secondary to the buildings and be rendered with "corresponding simplicity, formality, and dignity."

Less dramatic than their father's style, the landscape design by the younger Olmsteds called for a mostly geometric set of walkways, with hardwood trees such as elms lining the arteries. The ocular center of the main quad served as meeting point for the primary paths. The courts of Hutchinson Commons and Snell-Hitchcock Halls had sunken gardens crisscrossed by paved walks, which enhanced the cloistered effect of Cobb's plan. The Olmsted design also preserved unimpeded axial views across the interlocking quadrangles of the four-block site.

Significantly, the Olmsteds' landscape allowed for freedom of movement as well. Secondary paths meandered in a manner associated more strongly with Olmsted and Vaux. Botany Pond, on the edge of Hull Court, added a naturalized series of pools. The pond had an academic purpose as well as a decorative one: it became a study garden where the esteemed botanist John Coulter could experiment with rare specimens from around the world. Botany Pond no longer serves its scientific function, but it remains a vivid microcosm of biodiversity populated by dragonflies, turtles, mallards, and even tomcats in addition to the plant life.

THE COURTYARD (*right*) between Bartlett Gymnasium and Regenstein Library, once a parking lot, is planted with paperbark maple and crabapple trees. Magnolias in front of Bartlett (*left*) bloom for a few weeks every spring.

BOTANY POND (*pages 50–51*), Olmsted Brothers, ca. 1901. The pond, a biological microcosm, was originally a laboratory for scientists working in the Erman Biology Center.

THE ARTS AND CRAFTS INFLUENCE

As the decades passed, the university expanded, trees grew, limestone aged, and the campus acquired the timeless feel that its architects and designers sought. But it also changed more abruptly over time, and not always for the better. In the 1920s, excavations were ubiquitous as new steam tunnels were put in, not a high point for landscaping. And there was the effect of the automobile, with every opening between buildings being evaluated as a potential driveway.

Then in 1929, an interest in restoring a more bucolic environment led to a contract with the landscape gardener Beatrix Farrand. She had worked at other Gothic revival campuses, notably Princeton and Yale. Her light touch was informed by Arts and Crafts principles, which valued native materials, unconventional forms, and plantings that appeared as "inevitable" natural companions to buildings. The goal was for landscapes and architecture to look as though they had been in place for a long time.

Farrand's master plan, which she submitted to the university in 1932, took a middle course between the formality of the Olmsteds' 1902 plan and the asymmetry of a naturalized landscape. Her initial approach was to eliminate the circle in the main quad and to crisscross the quads generally with a fretwork of secondary walks, essentially creating small garden cells within the larger framework. Many of Farrand's ideas, including this one, were not executed, and they would have impeded vehicular access had they been adopted. But her planting suggestions were largely followed. Allées of honey locusts (some of which still exist) framed promenades. Native trees such as downy hawthorns appeared as natural entryways to buildings. Her vision also reached beyond the campus walls into the surrounding neighborhoods, as she exhorted faculty to select plantings for their homes as carefully as the university did for the campus.

Moreover, Farrand advised the university to grow its own plant material, both to economize and to encourage indigenous native species in the Arts and Crafts spirit. She explained that the work of landscaping, even the moving of trees around campus, was never ending. And, she insisted, the work should be organized so as to inspire enthusiasm among those hired to carry it out. "The spirit of a group of men is upheld by the sense that they are steadily employed in a worthwhile endeavour. The main key group of plantsmen should have continuing and, if possible, continuous work." Her remark underscored the principle that architecture and gardens are living things that cleave to the rhythms of the people who live and work there.

THE PLANS' ENDURING INFLUENCE

While most works of bricks and mortar make permanent (or at least long-term) marks on a campus, university master plans and especially landscaping are eminently changeable as time passes. Thus, the continuing impact of the university's early decisions and designs is remarkable.

Outdoor space and seamlessly woven planted gardens became key to the campus plan's success. Over the years, changes consistently have been informed by, and judged against, the broad outlines of the original plan. In 1958, one of Eero Saarinen's first university assignments was to create a new master plan, and his design, which was brilliant but largely ignored, represented broad variations on Henry Ives Cobb's theme.

THE OLMSTED BROTHERS' APPROACH to the campus at the beginning of the twentieth century was to create a landscape informed by both order and romance.

Saarinen's plan took the quadrangle approach seriously. He proposed the Midway campus as a new main axis, with traffic being rerouted to the south. A major building, unspecified, would enclose this mega-quadrangle at the east. Saarinen also drew in a major science quadrangle that would appear roughly along 58th Street (a feature that is only now being reconsidered).

In 1967, the architect Edward Larrabee Barnes drew a new plan for a so-called Student Village, an undergraduate complex with dormitories, music and theater venues, a museum, and a series of enclosed courtyards on the north edge of campus. The plan was only partly executed, as money was scarce and enrollments did not rise as expected. What was built—a high-rise dormitory, a museum, and a theater—did not meet expectations, less because of the buildings themselves than because they lacked the appealing outdoor spaces prevalent elsewhere on campus.

BOTANIC GARDEN IN THE CAMPUS

In the 1990s, the university successfully approached the American Public Garden Association for accreditation as a modern botanic garden. This move was made for several reasons, not least to help raise money specifically for the plantings on campus. Perhaps more important, the accreditation process instilled an awareness of plants and gardens throughout an institution that was profoundly, if not notoriously, decentralized. Little by little, plants and landscapes became a standard part of university design, and new building projects—such as the Hall for Economics—came to involve landscapes as artful as the buildings themselves.

A beautiful botanic garden resulted clearly from elements inherent in the university's original plan—the cloisterlike spaces, long axial vistas, and interlocking quadrangles. All have been sacred to generations of campus planners and architects. Such design continuity is rare. Landscape architect Richard Bumstead says the university's botanic garden is the envy of other institutions. As other university planners deal with the competing interests of the campus versus separate gardens or arboretums, he says, at the University of Chicago "they are one and the same."

TREES blooming in early spring enliven paths that lead in, out, and around the main quadrangle.

FOR A UNIVERSITY in the middle of a city, the University of Chicago campus is a special place. The campus is Gothic, so the eye is trained upward to the sky, our beautiful Midwestern sky.

I work in the Divinity School, which has a wonderful, soaring, towering atmosphere with big windows. In the summer, I watch the squirrels jumping from branch to branch. In the winter, wind, rain, and snow—everything is visible. It's not exactly like being out-of-doors, but it's very much open to the sky and to the trees and to the atmosphere, so I never feel claustrophobic, even if I work here all day long.

The Garden of the Mind

Comment by Wendy Doniger, Mircea Eliade Distinguished Service Professor

But I find that what sustains me is not just this building and the campus, but where the campus is situated.

To me, one of the privileges of our location is that we're so near Jackson Park, a picturesque place designed by Frederick Law Olmsted and Calvert Vaux. It has a lovely path and a fine lagoon and forest. I walk my dog at dawn every morning in Jackson Park, which is just across the Midway. It's right here. So our campus is not only urban, it has a piece of wildlife and of the country. If you get up early enough, you can see beavers in Jackson Park. The great blue herons are there most of the year. Geese too, and I've seen coyotes several times in Jackson Park, and once or twice I've seen a fox.

I think if I were just living in a building, however beautiful, I would get restless. But to have wildlife here as well is a real privilege.

To view a conversation with Professor Wendy Doniger, scan the QR code at left and select "Wendy Doniger."

WENDY DONIGER in her office in Swift Hall. A statue of Linné (*right*) stands in the winter garden of the Midway Plaisance.

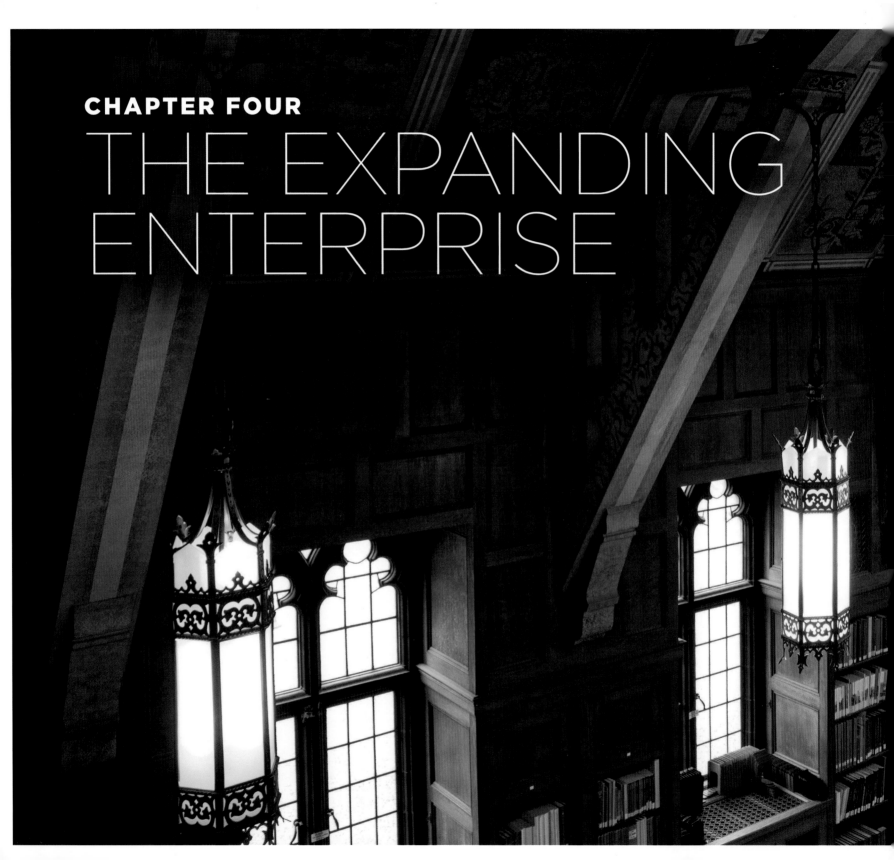

CHAPTER FOUR

THE EXPANDING ENTERPRISE

It is the best investment I ever made in my life.

— JOHN D. ROCKEFELLER

IN RELATIVELY SHORT ORDER, the University of Chicago realized the dreams of its founder and chief benefactor, and by the 1920s it possessed many marks of a first-rank university. Many of its scholars assumed national and international reputations. Perhaps most visibly, the university's ascent and ambition were evident in the expanding campus and in the stately character of its architecture.

The campus expansion required resources beyond Rockefeller's largesse and the founders' vision. In one of his last addresses to the university, on the occasion of his final $10 million gift, Rockefeller expressed his confidence that others would carry on the work of building a great institution. Donors' names on campus buildings—Billings, Culver, Eckhart, Noyes, Sunny, and Wieboldt, as well as trustees Rosenwald, Ryerson, and Swift—attest to the university's growing philanthropic partnerships. More important, a faculty with names such as Michelson in physics, Breasted in archaeology, and Dewey in education reflected a campus that was becoming a center for fearless intellectual inquiry.

THE READING ROOM of the Oriental Institute (*pages 60–61*), Mayers, Murray and Phillip, 1931.

ALBERT MERRITT BILLINGS HOSPITAL (*opposite*), Coolidge and Hodgdon, 1927. The architects adapted the Chicago Gothic template in the Medical Campus, using the quadrangle concept to create a courtyard that opened onto the Midway.

JAMES HENRY BREASTED

With the entrepreneurial zeal of both donors and scholars, the campus grew east and west, largely along the Midway on property that Rockefeller's money had purchased in 1906. Collectively they fulfilled the enduring vision of William Rainey Harper, who died that year. "Bran splinter new, yet solid as the ancient hills" was how Harper had described his concept of the university. The metaphor meant innovative research, rooted deeply in tradition. Not by chance, it also guided campus architecture, historical in look but modern in function.

ARCHITECTURE WITH A LAYERED PAST

The Oriental Institute provides a vivid example of the maturing university. Its 1931 building, housing a museum and the department of ancient Near Eastern history, represents the lifework of James Henry Breasted, whose career had begun some four decades earlier. When Harper was preparing to leave Yale for Chicago, he advised Breasted, who was finishing his master's at Yale that year, to obtain a doctorate in Berlin and then come to Chicago. A job would be waiting for him in Egyptology.

ORIENTAL INSTITUTE (*opposite and above*). The building's modern Gothic style was designed to accommodate the museum's mix of Art Deco detailing and ancient treasures. The newell post (*above right*) is a stylized version of the striding lion of Babylon. The cast of the Babylonian stela (*above*) records the Laws of Hammurabi.

Harper's faith in the young scholar was well placed. Breasted became a trailblazer in Near Eastern archaeology and authored a wide range of literature on the subject, from scholarly tracts to children's books. *Time* magazine pictured Breasted on its cover when the Oriental Institute opened its doors. Some say Steven Spielberg based the swashbuckling hero Indiana Jones on Breasted, though other models have been proposed, including another Oriental Institute archaeologist, Robert Braidwood.

Like many other early assets of the university, the Oriental Institute owed its existence directly to Rockefeller. The oil titan's first expression of interest in the ancient past came in a letter he sent to Breasted. Bearing a return address of The Homestead, Hot Springs, West Virginia, it was nearly mistaken for a vacation advertisement and tossed away. Luckily, Breasted opened the envelope and found Rockefeller's belated response to a request for funding.

The Oriental Institute's architects were from the office of the late Bertram Grosvenor Goodhue, architect of Rockefeller Chapel, which had been built on an adjacent site a few years before. Architecturally, both the chapel and the institute represent prime examples of the university's modern Gothic style. Both employ the complex massing common to medieval buildings—and to Gothic revival—but have exterior surfaces stripped to their taut, mostly unadorned skins. The Oriental Institute is smaller and less elaborate than the chapel, of course. But like the chapel, its smooth exterior is punctuated with simple carvings, in this case inspired by the ancient world: Turkey, Rome, and Assyria.

AERIAL VIEW OF CAMPUS, 1907.

In contrast to its exterior, the institute's interior exhibits the colorful and highly detailed ornamentation of Art Deco. The Deco touches can be seen in the generous amounts of Egyptian-like stenciling in a manner associated with "Egyptomania." This was a design craze brought on by the discovery of King Tutankhamun's tomb in 1922—an event in which Breasted himself played a central role. The geometric design of the gallery brass doors recall the gates to King Tut's tomb, opened when Breasted was brought in to mediate between the volatile discoverer of the tomb, Howard Carter, and his antagonistic financier, Lord Carnavon.

Breasted's ambition remains obvious in a building that became his lasting memorial. The winged-bull gate from Khorsabad in ancient Assyria, brought back by an expedition of Chicago archaeologists, had to be wheeled into place before the museum's wall could be completed. A statue of Tutankhamun and a granite bull's head from Persepolis figure prominently in an interior that represents twentieth-century fashion as much as it reaches back to the ancient world.

"THE HIGHEST IDEALS OF MEDICINE"

A larger architectural project on the west end of campus, under construction by the late 1920s, bore witness to the university's desire to unite its academic enterprise with the needs of the outside world. This was the medical complex, whose early buildings were designed by Coolidge and Hodgdon. Charles Coolidge had enjoyed a long history with

the university, dating back to 1900 when he accompanied Charles Hutchinson to Europe. Coolidge had headed the Boston firm of Shepley, Rutan and Coolidge, which conceived the Tower Group and Harper Library in the original quadrangles, largely in the image of Oxford and Cambridge. He eventually opened a Chicago office with an associate from Boston, Frederick Hodgdon, and they went on to design Swift Hall and George Herbert Jones Laboratory on the quads.

The construction of Albert Merritt Billings Hospital and Abbott Memorial Hall in 1927 represented the long-awaited fulfillment of an idea that Harper and the university founders had imagined almost from the beginning. Harper had been eager, perhaps overeager, to establish a medical department. He decided to form a relationship with Rush Medical College on the city's West Side, a move that may have been precipitate since Rockefeller, the university's biggest benefactor, believed that Rush was not of the university's caliber. Rockefeller responded by dramatically, though temporarily, withdrawing his support from the university.

Ultimately the university did establish its medical school and built Billings and Abbott as the original quadrangles had been built—with open space and room to grow. At the dedication of Billings, Yale president James Angell (formerly dean at Chicago) noted during his address that medicine was shedding the status of a trade along the lines of

"carpentry and plumbing" and other manual arts. "The preservation of the highest ideals of medicine is obviously one of the prime duties of civilization," Angell said.

Organizationally, the university linked medical research and clinical practice to the department of biology, and while the laboratories of Hull Court stayed put, Billings and Abbott were designed to express an unmistakable connection with the existing quadrangles, with the limestone and Gothic profile already prevalent on campus.

Coolidge and Hodgdon modified the quadrangle template by designing a courtyard in front of Billings, which opened onto the Midway and to the community that it served. Later hospital units, which would run along the Midway in both directions, were sited to retain courtyards within the medical center, both to echo the quad concept and to take advantage of natural light and fresh air. "Sunlight is now an acknowledged retardant, if not an actual destroyer, of micro-organisms, and it is highly desirable that sunlight shall enter almost every part of an institution," explained an authoritative book on hospital design coauthored by Richard Schmidt, who would design the Chicago Lying-In Hospital beside Billings in 1930.

By World War II, the study and practice of medicine had advanced, and expanding hospital departments required the construction of new wings. The open spaces of the courtyards became a bygone luxury on this part of campus, as quadrangles shrank and cloisters became beehives. Patient care became hermetically sealed from outside elements, eventually with air conditioning and glass curtain walls, and the need for courtyards diminished further.

SOUTH CAMPUS: THE FIRST MIDWAY CROSSING

While the University of Chicago campus acquired a richness that reflected the university's reputation, there remained a significant lack of facilities for student residential life. "We like to believe that a spirit of friendliness and mutual interest pervades the Quadrangles," wrote Frederic C. Woodward, vice president and dean of faculties, in 1927. Recognizing "the fundamental importance . . . of habitual discussion outside the classroom," Woodward lamented the fact that only "a small minority" of students lived in dormitories on campus. He led the charge for expanded

living quarters, and an ambitious plan was devised, nearly as large as the original quads, just south of the Midway.

Architect Charles Z. Klauder of Philadelphia rendered an elaborate scheme for college housing, sparing no detail in creating a French Gothic village ("French Gothic" being Klauder's term for styling with rich roofline ornamentation) of twelve courtyards and a three-hundred-foot tower between Woodlawn and Ellis Avenues. Klauder had designed dormitories at Princeton, Cornell, and the University of Pennsylvania, and he would later design Eckhart Hall for the mathematics department. When he delivered his beautiful drawing of "The College of the University," he estimated its price at $12.5 million, and the trustees balked. They told him that they chiefly wanted residence halls. The library and classroom buildings included in the scheme could wait.

Aside from finances, other significant forces conspired against the South Campus project. A powerful faculty group resisted any expansion of undergraduate facilities whatsoever, believing that such expansion could come only at the expense of graduate-based research. "Let undergraduate loafers go anywhere else, especially to Yale and Harvard where swaggy manners and curious accents can be learned easily," wrote history professor William Dodd, who preferred the university's role as a serious research institution.

By 1931, the first and only phase of the residence project, Burton-Judson Courts, was built at the corner of 60th Street and Ellis Avenue, largely with money from Sears, Roebuck

To view a video of Philip Enquist of Skidmore, Owings and Merrill discussing plans for South Campus, scan the QR code at left and select "Philip Enquist."

owner Julius Rosenwald. It was designed by another Philadelphia firm, Zantzinger, Borie and Medary, in a rich Gothic revival manner. Like other modern Gothic buildings of the period, it is devoid of the oriels, crockets, and gargoyles that adorn earlier buildings on the quads. Yet the construction is hardly stark. Variegated stone gives the exterior surface liveliness. Courtyards are ample. Perhaps most important, the interiors of carved wood and cathedral-like common rooms were designed to be luxurious and were advertised to the headmasters of Eastern prep schools as comparable to the residences at Ivy League schools.

THE LAB SCHOOLS

As the growing university built new buildings beyond the original quadrangles, academic initiatives increasingly involved the community in Hyde Park and neighborhoods in the area. Among these were the Laboratory Schools, which educated children in castlelike buildings situated east along the Midway. Around the turn of the century, Harper had commissioned James Gamble Rogers to design two of the school buildings, Emmons Blaine Hall and Henry Holmes Belfield Hall, largely in line with Cobb's template but possessing their own character. The Lab Schools taught according to the principles of John Dewey, who founded the schools and stressed creativity as essential to learning. Consequently, the buildings were designed with a view to their effect on children. Such buildings should have "a well defined retired character," wrote Rogers, which translated into architecture of substantial symmetry and restrained complexity.

By the 1920s, the Lab Schools had entered a golden age in which the community shared the school's views and the student body became known for its diversity and achievement. New structures went up in this period, reflecting the schools' confidence and pride. Sunny Gymnasium, built in 1929, resolved an old problem for the high school (called University High) basketball team, which had been forced to shoot baskets low and fast because of the stunted ceiling in the old facility. The Chicago firm of Armstrong, Furst and Tilton, known mostly as church architects, endowed the new gym with a luxuriously carved

Gothic design—a sign that the Lab Schools, which were largely independent, identified with the university. Charles Hubbard Judd Hall, designed by the same firm, went up between Blaine and Belfield and represented one of the two most delicately detailed Gothic revival buildings on campus. (Eckhart was the other.) These flourishes came, perhaps ironically, just as the university's love affair with all things Gothic was in its final throes.

WHAT, NO GOTHIC?

The architectural style that had dominated the University of Chicago since its founding lost popularity during the Depression and World War II. Gothic's vaunted use of handcrafts was no longer valued in the machine age, and its artisanal stonecutting and stone carving eventually yielded to the demand for mass production. The Bauhaus became the epitome of the new architectural style called modernism. Change was nigh.

The Administration Building, built in 1948, became the university's first foray in the modern direction. Intended to meet a long-standing need to consolidate offices for the president and other institutional managers, it would occupy one of the last vacant spaces

on the quadrangles. Gothic designs for the building were floated, but progressive critics were quick to deride the medieval template as obsolete and expensive. The university magazine complained that a recent renovation of Goodspeed Hall cost more than its original construction some fifty years before. The same writer found flaws in other Gothic buildings, such as the "impractical" greenhouse atop Culver and the lighting scheme in Harper Library's reading room, which, he said, still baffled illumination engineers.

Early credit for the anti-Gothic style of the Administration Building may go to local doyenne Carroll Mason Russell and her husband, trustee Peter Russell. Carroll Russell wrote in her 1982 memoir that the modern movement at the university effectively commenced when the couple heard Joseph Hudnut, Harvard's architecture dean, preach the modernist message at a lecture downtown. History was dead in architecture, Hudnut said. Gothic and the like were irrelevant to modern life. The Russells, hardly fire-breathing progressives, were converted, and Peter Russell was sufficiently powerful to impose the new stripped-down style on Holabird, Root and Burgee, the firm designing the administrative offices.

The Administration Building became not only the largest structure on the quads but also the one with the least detail, inside and out. It was unloved from the beginning. One alumnus pined for the Gothic buildings of old, stating, "I shall never forget my first glimpse of the pinnacles of Cobb and Harper rising majestically." Another hoped that university botanists might invent a method of making the ivy outside the building grow rapidly "so as to conceal [the building's architecture] so far as possible, and as quickly as possible."

Whether the Administration Building is regrettable or a sign of its time remains a matter of taste. It does have luxuriant ivy, and it is framed by colorful gardens when perennials are in season. When president Hanna Holborn Gray occupied the building, she reportedly declared that its businesslike profile suited its function and properly distinguished it from the Gothic academic buildings. President Gray did not need to add that Chicago's Gothic revival, also excoriated over the years, had steadfastly withstood the test of time.

ADMINISTRATION BUILDING, Holabird, Root and Burgee, 1948. Situated in the main quadrangle, the modernist Admin Building drew controversy when it was built.

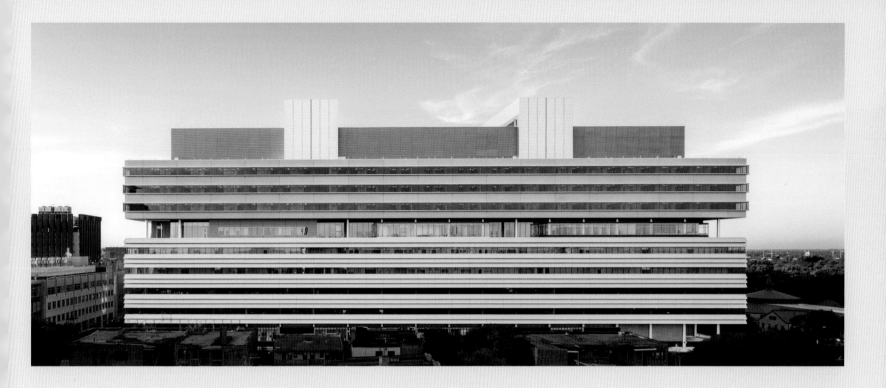

At the Forefront: Rafael Viñoly

THE CENTER FOR CARE AND DISCOVERY, the second campus building designed by Rafael Viñoly, is a surprise. Not for its architectural pyrotechnics, but for its economy.

The new building is massive but otherwise not eye-catching in profile. Its genius is in its inner measurements: an unflinchingly regular grid of bays set inside an orthogonal box.

Restrained architecture is not boring architecture, however, and Viñoly's box remains a striking work, particularly for its interior of interlocking space, transparency, and human scale. Its immensity is broken down by the geometry of its parts, a quality for which Viñoly is particularly proud. In this respect, the architect invokes Frank Lloyd Wright, whose Robie House, not large, sits directly across the street from Viñoly's Chicago School of Business's Harper Center. which fills most of a city block.

"What the Robie House does is fundamentally investigate the one thing that I think unifies all architecture," Viñoly says, "which is the phenomenally subtle play of proportions and scale."

To view a video of Rafael Viñoly discussing plans for the Center for Care and Discovery, scan the QR code at left and select "Rafael Viñoly–CCD."

CHAPTER FIVE

EMBRACING MIDCENTURY MODERNISM

Universities are to our time what the monasteries were to the Middle Ages, oases in our desert-like civilization. They have about the only pedestrian spaces that are left to us. And it may turn out that they have our only permanent architecture.

—EERO SAARINEN

IN THE ECONOMIC BOOM of the 1950s, on campuses and almost everyplace else, modernist and often radical building design quickly displaced the familiar styles of the past. After the Depression and the war, serious architecture had assumed the unornamented and often terse profile that had been imported from Europe. Midcentury modernism ("modernism" as distinguished from the perennially evolving "modern") represented a myriad of styles using glass and steel and reinforced concrete. The palette did not include Gothic revival.

"The battle of modern architecture has been won," wrote Eero Saarinen, the great modernist who in 1955 was hired by the university, his first and only client in Chicago proper. Modernism, with its emphasis on large-scale planning, simple lines, and machine-wrought materials, promised needed changes on campus quickly and economically. The administration hoped that in Saarinen's hands—he had done planning and building designs at MIT, Yale, and elsewhere—the changes would be executed with artfulness but also thrift.

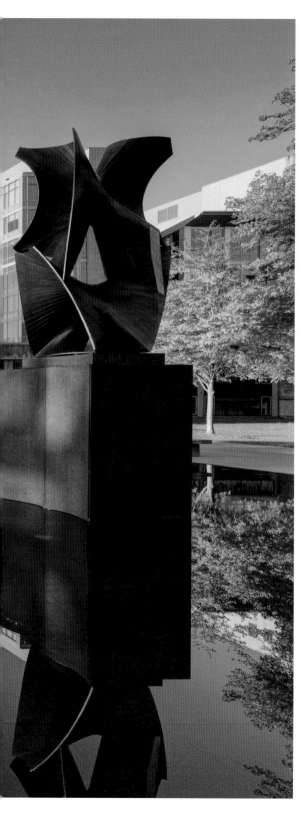

THE HARMONIOUS PAST AND FUTURE

The selection of Saarinen, initially to do a master plan, indicated the university's understanding that despite the shift away from history, its existing architecture represented a precious asset. Saarinen, one of the two or three most important modernist architects in the world at the time, seemed uniquely willing to harmonize the new with the old. (In contrast, Mies van der Rohe was famously indifferent to the other buildings in his midst.) Saarinen's father, Eliel, gave his son valuable advice to work by: "Always look at the next larger thing." In designing a building, consider the campus at large. In planning a campus, consider the city around it.

Saarinen had immense respect for the Chicago campus. In an article for *Architectural Record*, he marveled at Hutchinson Court's "beautiful, harmonious" Gothic buildings, the work of three different (sometimes competing) architects. He also took a swipe at his fellow modernists: "Imagine what would have happened if three or four equally eminent architects were asked in our day to do the four sides of a square!" Saarinen was a modernist but no radical, and the university trusted him to treat its architectural past with care.

Over a period of four or five years, Saarinen produced a series of master plans that proposed courts and quadrangles much in the spirit of Cobb's original. One of his plans even used the Midway itself as the university's main axis and university green. He also designed the Laird Bell Law Quadrangle, built in 1959, and the now-razed Woodward Court dormitories, built the previous year. Saarinen died in 1961 at the age of fifty-one and did not have the opportunity to see all of his plans through. But what is left of his work, the Law School, is a masterpiece that reflects an understanding of the campus that few other architects demonstrated.

LAIRD BELL LAW QUADRANGLE, Eero Saarinen and Associates, 1959. *Construction in Space in the Third and Fourth Dimension* by Antoine Pevsner (1959), stands as the centerpiece of the Law School's reflecting pool.

"NOR MUST WE BECOME TIMID"

Saarinen won the Law School commission only after a series of other architects were dismissed. "The law faculty didn't feel that the other architects were listening to them," remembers Kent Cooper, an architect in Saarinen's firm who worked on the project from design through construction. The law complex, sometimes called the "eighth quadrangle" in reference to Cobb's original seven, harmonized with the old campus, but not by imitating it. Rather, Saarinen blended modernist conventions with subtle but defining characteristics of the Gothic campus.

Several elements of the Law School design are predictable enough, such as the open-ended courtyard and broad views across the Midway. Saarinen designed long, low classroom and administrative wings, in keeping with the modernist interest in horizontality and interlocking space (also favored by Frank Lloyd Wright and Mies van der Rohe). The buildings were clad in the same Indiana limestone used in their Gothic brethren. The nearby fountain and plantings, by modernist landscape architect Dan Kiley, softened the lines without upsetting the Mondrianesque order.

THE STRENGTH OF SAARINEN'S INTERIORS is in their simple structure and timeless proportions. In the most recent of a series of renovations, completed in 2008, the Green Room (*opposite*) was decorated with modernist paintings and furniture. The reading room of the D'Angelo Law Library (*right*) was renovated with floating balconies and low-iron plate glass.

What was surprising and ingenious was the central element, the D'Angelo Law Library. Modern architects should "express in our architecture that we are living in a new era," Saarinen wrote. "Nor must we become timid just in order to preserve unity." The D'Angelo was anything but timid. The six-story tower represented a vertical counterpoint to the horizontal wings, its pleated glass made with a technology (neoprene seals) developed by another Saarinen client, General Motors. The tower's sawtooth roofline represented an abstract reference to the gabled Gothic dormitory, Burton-Judson, next door.

When it was finished, critics praised the Law School for its unlikely harmony with older neighbors. The faculty was less thrilled. Interiors were rudimentary, offices were not ample, and the "airport style" seating in the student lounge did not encourage conversation. The building served well enough for several decades, but in the 1980s there was talk of abandoning it and building anew elsewhere on campus.

Instead, the faculty concluded that the Law School had character worth saving, especially its unique layout, with faculty offices encircling the library. Plus, it was designed by Saarinen, a recognized master. So the school embarked on a series of renovations,

THE SCHOOL OF SOCIAL SERVICE ADMINISTRATION (*pages 86–87 and above*). The building challenges the notion that Miesian architecture is out-of-place on the time-honored campus. Its split levels and interior finishes bear the hallmark of midcentury Mies, yet its precise geometry complements the patterns inherent in Gothic architecture.

endowing the building with features that Saarinen might have included originally if he had had the resources. They changed furniture and wall finishes. They improved classrooms. Notably, they pushed the south wall out twenty-five feet, an addition that Saarinen quite probably did not anticipate. But his building's precise geometry, which was essential to its graceful blending with the existing campus in 1959, was exactly what enabled architects to enlarge it with seamless harmony nearly three decades later.

THE INEVITABLE MODERN

As new architecture developed all over the country, it was sometimes motivated by forces other than the artistic preferences of prominent architects. Economic or social needs were sometimes more urgent. At the edges of campus at midcentury, the university engineered a massive effort in urban renewal, to purchase and remove decayed property and build something new. Modernism had been promoted as a functional, rationalist approach to architecture, one that was well suited to large projects. Thus the style was naturally embraced for the declining neighborhood that the university and the city were trying to save.

Rows of economically designed townhouses, many of which would house university employees, were built along the edge of campus. University Park Towers—an early work by I. M. Pei—bisected 55th Street. The buildings won plaudits for saving the neighborhood from encroaching slums. Yet the new development also prompted some regret for having replaced Hyde Park's diverse street life with buildings that made a virtue of bland repetition. Urban renewal provided a cautionary tale about architecture that strove for simplicity but also risked widespread tedium.

MIES VAN DER ROHE'S ECCENTRIC GEM

In contrast to the architecture of urban renewal, midcentury buildings on campus have stood the test of time. For these buildings, the university commissioned some of the country's leading modernists. Most eminent of all was Ludwig Mies van der Rohe, who designed the School of Social Service Administration two doors down from the Law School. This commission came about at the behest of Lillian Greenwald, the widow of developer Herbert Greenwald, who had been Mies's most important patron and a prominent SSA donor.

JOSEPH REGENSTEIN LIBRARY, Skidmore, Owings and Merrill (Walter Netsch, designer), 1970. The Regenstein represents a bridge between the campus's old architecture and the modern.

Unlike Saarinen's Law School, the classically Miesian SSA building, predictably low slung and transparent, made no attempt to adapt to the surroundings. In some ways, SSA benefits from the partial horizontality of the Law School nearby, as does another prominent building of the period located down the street, the School of Continuing Education (later renovated as the New Graduate Residence Hall), designed by another famous modernist, Edward Durell Stone.

While Mies's SSA building seems heedless of the vertical dominance of the rest of the campus, the university's only building by one of the century's great architects represents a pristine and self-contained work of art that would command a presence no matter where it was sited. It can be perceived less as a horizontal building than one that defies gravity in the way its floors float within the spare steel frame. It has no courtyard, but the large glass lobby of the building creates an unmistakably protected space. It also does what quadrangles do elsewhere on campus, which is to open itself to distant views, in this case across the Midway. That such an ostensibly simple box should engender such a complex set of perceptions is what made Mies arguably the most influential (and hard to imitate) architect of the modernist era.

REGENSTEIN LIBRARY: THE "QUIET GIANT"

As more new buildings became necessary on campus, and as Gothic revival remained out of the question, the university faced the complicated proposition of how to incorporate modernism, given all its forms and iterations. If the previous century had involved a war of styles (largely between the classical and the Gothic), the modernist vocabulary was chaotic with "isms" such as brutalism, rationalism, expressionism, and Miesianism. The successful harmony of midcentury architecture at the university is a testament to the planners who sited the buildings as well as the skill of the architects involved.

It was no surprise that the hardest building to assimilate was the largest. For Joseph Regenstein Library, completed in 1970, questions of scale were troublesome from the beginning. Early schemes for a structure to house 1.8 million volumes sited it at the open east end of the main quadrangles, on University Avenue across from the Oriental Institute. This corresponded generally to Cobb's original plan, to enclose the quads with buildings that included a mammoth library. But needs had grown in a half-century, and a library

at this site above ground would have also required two basements running the length of the main quadrangle to the steps of the Administration Building. To avoid this kind of disruption, planners followed an earlier Saarinen master plan that situated the library at the old Stagg Field.

In selecting an architect for Regenstein, the "quiet giant," administrators and donors "chose an enormous firm for an enormous job" when they hired Skidmore, Owings and Merrill, wrote the *Maroon*. Regarded as heir to the Miesian glass-and-steel aesthetic, SOM designed Sears Tower and the John Hancock building in this period. But instead of an oversized glass container for books, the firm's lead designer, Walter Netsch, proposed a brutalist masonry design that was inspired by the existing Gothic template. Netsch had become famous for his design of the Air Force Academy in Colorado Springs and its starkly geometric chapel, which rises in brilliant, if shocking, counterpoint to the mountains behind it.

Netsch promised that Regenstein would "not dominate the area" and would be "responsive to the park plan." He spoke of the "negative spaces," voids in the mass of the building. The outer wall of the library would project and recede, create partial courtyards, and introduce the play of light and shadow in the manner of Gothic architecture.

The question, of course, was how to accomplish this in the boxy modernist style. For Netsch, the answer lay in an approach that he called field theory. This aesthetic allowed Netsch and his followers to compose large, complex buildings out of simple geometric units. Significantly, Netsch often talked about the inspiration of field theory in Gothic architecture, citing Chartres. "What was important to me was . . . that it had been built over time and still had order," he said. "The Gothic form, this soaring form, the complex geometry," largely inspired the geometries of field theory.

Yet, field theory was hard to understand no matter who was explaining it. In a 1990 article, the magazine *Inland Architect* attempted to illustrate the idea, and began the essay with the waggish warning, "Kids, don't try this at home without proper supervision." Field theory could achieve immeasurable complexity by simply rotating squares and superimposing them on one another. Floor plans and elevations could resemble crystalline minerals, the idea being that crystals grow at random but have an immutable underlying order. Field theory enabled the simple and repetitive unit of the square to assume infinitely varied forms.

REGENSTEIN (*opposite and above*) was shocking when new. Its jagged massing, courtyards between asymmetrical parts, and the never-twice-the-same cut of its limestone make the library a striking brutalist interpretation of Gothic motifs.

Netsch's later buildings would be designed in ways that defied right angles. Regenstein might have done that too, except that the university's head librarian, Herman Fussler, insisted that the stack areas on five floors remain traditionally orthogonal (unlike other, more confusing libraries designed by Netsch). Ultimately the eccentric geometry of off-center cubes holds to cardinal directions, and Regenstein has gained the affection of those who use it. The structure's big limestone blocks blend nicely in scale and tone with Gothic revival neighbors.

As with the best buildings on campus, Regenstein also represents an example of architecture that has aged gracefully. At first it suffered (or, perhaps, benefited) from the "shock of the new," its modern brutalism a direct challenge to the quads' intricately carved exterior facades. The fortresslike aspect seemed inimical to the almost ecclesiastical delicacy of the earlier buildings.

But time is the friend of good architecture. The library's rugged protrusions and setbacks have been softened by familiarity and lush plantings. Sidewalk critics laud the "raked," or deeply etched, limestone, which gives the surface a handmade feel. More recently, Netsch's library design was affirmed by the creation of a lovely new quadrangle formed on three sides by Regenstein, with Bartlett Dining Commons and Max Palevsky Residential Commons. The beauty of this grassy interlude proves the importance of scale, asymmetry, interlocking space, and careful geometry in a campus with a history too long and a character too varied to be contained in any one style.

THE UNIVERSITY OF CHICAGO is a destination for people coming to visit the city, in part because of the architecture. The campus architecture looms large in Chicago.

Mies van der Rohe's Social Service Administration building alone is worth a trip to campus—that's a very good building. Eero Saarinen's Law School, while a period piece, was a brilliant tour de force of its time, no question. I think Helmut Jahn's three buildings—the Joe and Rika Mansueto Library and the west and south utility plants—will be among the panoply of buildings to see. And Tod Williams and Billie Tsien's Logan Center for the Arts is superlative, first class. So are Jamie Carpenter's beautiful light standards on the midway, the Midway Crossings. They are spectacular, I mean utterly spectacular.

Destination UChicago

Comment by Stanley Tigerman, Principal, Tigerman McCurry Architects

Other buildings, as nature has a wonderful way of ameliorating and softening them, will find their place. It's good the university never forced new architecture to be contextual with older buildings. Each building is of its time. Some might say that creates a mishmash; I don't think so. It shows a real honesty in trying to build contemporary buildings.

To view a video of Stanley Tigerman discussing the new Seminary Co-op Bookstore, scan the QR code at left and select "Stanley Tigerman."

CHAPTER SIX

THE ARCHITECTURE
OF SCIENCE

Laboratory buildings are like Gothic cathedrals, which in medieval Europe represented the pinnacle of science . . . this idea that you could make stone climb to the sky and fill the spaces in between with colored glass to illustrate your conception of the Universe, and inspire people to do great things.

— JEFF SCHANTZ, Architect

AT ALMOST ANY MODERN RESEARCH UNIVERSITY, new buildings designed for science are among the largest and most prominent on campus. Generous funding to pay for such buildings is offered through private and public sources, which are dedicated to the miracles of biomedicine, for instance, and the wonders of nanotechnology. But the grandeur of these buildings is not just a matter of money. Dramatic architecture also reflects the spirit of scientific inquiry, the free and open exchange of ideas taking place in exuberant, light-filled buildings.

The Knapp Center for Biomedical Discovery, completed in 2009, follows just such a contemporary template. It is constructed mostly of glass, with laboratories largely open inside and interior walls, when called for, usually transparent. The crystalline nature of the building could hardly be more different from the cell-like quarters that solitary scientists once occupied. Knapp's ten stories sit on a partly limestone base, which blends reasonably well with the Gothic buildings of the neighborhood. But the past is largely forgotten in the glass tower that rises luminously over the local skyline.

KNAPP CENTER's open spaces allow scientists to relax, interact, and discuss common problems.

Knapp almost gleefully proclaims modernity, but there are practical reasons for housing laboratories in glass as well. Transparency encourages researchers to interact and cross over into other disciplines besides their own—in this case fields as diverse as computation, biophysics, genomics, and pediatrics. To facilitate this interaction, a series of double-story light courts run up the north end of the building, spacious places for relaxing and chatting over coffee. These sky lobbies are intended for those wanting to break away from the labs and benches inside, but with balconies overhead and views of the city, they also inspire meetings and reflect activity of another kind. The form-follows-function objective of this and other spaces in Knapp is to foster collaboration. It enables a cross-pollination of ideas and the creation of scientific insight as advanced as the architecture at hand.

THE MODERN FAITH IN SCIENCE

Architecture's role in science at the university is not a new one. Kent Chemical Laboratory on the main quad represented one of Henry Ives Cobb's most stately exteriors on the early campus, reflecting the importance of the work within. President Harper explained why the building was significant. "A century ago there was really no such thing as science," he wrote. But science had since become a touchstone addressing "everything, from God Himself to the most insignificant atom of His Creation."

Reinforcing the importance of science a few years later, Helen Culver, donor

of the biology buildings on Hull Court, spoke at the 1897 opening of the zoology, physiology, anatomy, and botany buildings. "I have believed that moral evils would grow less as knowledge of their relation to physical life prevails—and that science, which is knowing, knowing the truth, is a foundation of pure religion." Indeed, the labs that she paid for, with carved limestone and ornate arcades linking the structures, conceded nothing to the more time-honored fields of history and theology.

The architecture of science buildings changed, not always for the better, as the role of science changed in American culture. In the 1940s, Professor Enrico Fermi's Manhattan Project team labored in a makeshift laboratory under the stands of abandoned Stagg Field. The secret project took place within the environs of a fortresslike structure, with medieval-looking towers capped by battlements. The stadium's architecture became an unintended symbol of the nuclear age in 1942 with Chicago Pile 1 (CP-1) and the first controlled self-sustaining nuclear reaction, which proved the feasibility of nuclear energy.

Physicists expressed themselves more openly—though not more elaborately—when the Enrico Fermi and James Franck Institutes (for nuclear research and the study of metals, respectively) were built in 1948. In the postwar economic and scientific boom, money was available to build labs and continue atomic research for peaceful purposes. Significant funding came from private industry, motivated by the belief that technical discoveries could be readily transferred to commercial development.

The institutes represented cultural and scientific steps forward, and it was natural to expect distinguished, even progressive, architectural designs for them. Professors George Marmont and Robert Moon penned a "Desiderata for a Space to House a Community of Scientists," which included sketches of a building similar to Frank Lloyd Wright's Johnson Wax Headquarters in Racine, Wisconsin. But it was not to be. Ultimately, the institutes were designed as simple rectangles made of limestone cut to resemble concrete, with unremarkable floor plans.

HENRY MOORE: CREATING SACRED SPACE

Ultimately it was sculpture rather than architecture that first conveyed the power and hopes for Fermi's science in the future. When Stagg Field was demolished, a committee consisting of art professor Harold Haydon, history professor William McNeill, and university architect I. W. Colburn contacted Henry Moore, the English sculptor, to produce what became an iconic work in bronze, *Nuclear Energy.* Installed on Ellis Avenue in 1967, the twelve-foot sculpture had undeniable impact on almost anyone who saw it.

WILLIAM ECKHARDT RESEARCH CENTER, HOK, completion 2015.

"One might think of the lower part of it being protective . . . and constructed for human beings and the top being more like the idea of the destructive side to the atom," Moore explained. "So between the two, it might express to people, in some symbolic way, the whole event."

The area around the sculpture has assumed the air of sacred space. In subsequent decades, major buildings have been organized around the sculpture, including the William Eckhardt Research Center, which replaced the Fermi and Franck institutes and where physics would be studied in the twenty-first century. In its own way, Moore's work helped bring the subject of nuclear physics fully out in the open. At the university if not elsewhere, laboratory buildings would become more symbolic henceforth.

NUCLEAR ENERGY, Henry Moore, bronze, 1967.

THE DAWN OF MODERN BIOMEDICINE

Not long after the dawn of the nuclear era came a revolution in biomedical science. At the University of Chicago, the pioneering use of chemical agents to treat cancer and the development of nuclear imaging and radiation oncology were changing research and clinical agendas. University planners responded by expanding infrastructure to house these new branches of science.

In the 1960s, I. W. Colburn was named the university architect, and he designed buildings that attempted to reflect the complex role of science in society. "Modern architecture has always denied the emotional dimension and has appealed only to [the] intellect," he wrote (somewhat forgetting the expressiveness of Hull Court). "A mature architect should be concerned with man's grace, glory, and aspirations as achieved though the traditional manipulation of space, color and light."

Colburn's designs for the Henry Hinds Laboratory for Geophysical Sciences and the Cummings Life Science Center were noted at the time not only for their brutalist profiles but also for their abstract references to the Gothic. There are many ways of interpreting Cummings in particular—an eleven-story modernist tower whose laboratory ventilation is concealed behind vertical brick stacks that rise above the roofline, where they resemble battlements overlooking the realm.

CUMMINGS
represents an essay in
brutalism, with brick
stacks, concealing
laboratory ventilation,
rising to form a
castellated parapet.

HENRY HINDS LABORATORY FOR GEOPHYSICAL SCIENCES (*right*), I. W. Colburn, 1967. The towers, which house elevators, plumbing stacks, and ventilation, represent a midcentury take on the university's medievalism. Ceramic murals (*above*), by Ruth Duckworth, decorate the entry.

The towers of Cummings and Hinds may be likened to those of castles protecting hill towns. But the ponderous architecture achieved something more than putting modern function inside vaguely medieval profiles. These buildings became parts of a new science quadrangle, considered the ninth quadrangle (after the seven original ones plus the Law School).

In 1984, the John Crerar Library was built along the west edge of this open space. It was designed as another brutalist essay, if a less conspicuous one, with recessed openings under a massing of cantilevered limestone. One can hardly look at it today without recalling the thick walls, architectural and otherwise, that once existed between scientists and the public. Yet it incorporates a more felicitous note of modernity inside, with its glass atrium opening to the sky. This feature brings natural light to the interior, helping to illuminate those floors devoted to open shelving of books.

QUADRANGLE BY ACCRETION

The science quad grew in form and character with the Kersten Physics Teaching Center, completed in 1985. The building's exterior is a study in contrast. The side along Ellis Avenue is faced with limestone ashlar and recessed windows, like the campus buildings of old, as if protecting the scientists within from the gaze of the outside world. The portion facing the quad, however, presents a facade almost unrestrained in its use of glass, fairly beckoning the world to look inside. Curtain walls and broad terraces with glass doors reflect what can only be interpreted as openness and a love of daylight—as well as a foreshadowing of building designs to come.

The architecture of science closely follows changes in research methods. The Gordon

JOHN CRERAR LIBRARY (*above, at left*), Stubbins Associates, 1984. Kersten and Crerar, along with the later Gordon Center (*above, at right*), form the perimeter of the "ninth quadrangle," which serves the university's sciences.

Center for Integrative Science, built in 2005, typifies the trend in the most modern laboratories today, with glass walls inside and out and otherwise minimal barriers between people and disciplines. The design of the prominent Boston-based architectural firm Ellenzweig emphasizes, with abundant common areas and open space, the interaction among scientists that takes place within.

Gordon Center—shared by biology, chemistry, and physics—features large, open labs and light-filled atriums. Glass lobbies visually overlap with the adjacent outdoor space, all encouraging researchers in different branches of science to cross paths. The building expresses the conviction that discoveries will come when scientists from different fields address common problems together.

GORDON CENTER FOR INTEGRATIVE SCIENCE, Ellenzweig, 2005. Tucked among other medical buildings, the Gordon Center unites the biological and physical sciences in an interdisciplinary research environment.

The Gordon Center's design is as modern as its function, yet the architects were careful to acknowledge the traditional neighborhood as well. The construction features its share of limestone walls, which suggest stability and connection with the old campus. But its main entrance—a contemporary porte-cochere held aloft by six-story steel columns—is as open and celebratory in its own way as old Cobb Gate less than a block away. Moreover, the Gordon Center encloses the science quadrangle and creates a dominant sight line through its gate and across open space, terminating at the carved stone arch of Abbott Memorial Hall on the other side of 58th Street. The alignment had been planned for years and neatly expresses the university's blend of diversity and continuity.

DESIGNING FOR CREATIVE INSIGHT

In 2011, the university held a conference on the role of architecture in the conduct of science, with architects and scientists discussing how design encourages discovery. As one panelist observed, though, the relationship between the two professions was not always a close one. He recalled that in the 1970s, "money spent on architecture [was considered] money not spent on science." That attitude gradually changed, and today research is conducted in dramatic modern structures all over America.

Steve Wiesenthal, the university's chief architect, remarked at the time that buildings can "create environments that are evermore conducive to sparks of creative insight." Wiesenthal allowed that architecture and science are characteristically different, in many ways opposite. Nevertheless, science itself had begun to measure the effects of different physical environments on the creative mind. And architecture is insatiable for new information, new ideas, that can be incorporated into an innovative design.

When the conference was held, the university was in the midst of designing what may become its most advanced laboratory, the Eckhardt Center, for fields of study ranging from high energy physics to molecular engineering. The architecture firm of HOK was in the process of designing this sculptural, unabashedly transparent building across the street from Mansueto and the Henry Moore sculpture and within sight of the old quads. If there was a building suitable for tapping into the humanistic side of science, this was it.

To design Eckhardt, the university chose the firm of HOK, whose principals Bill Odell and Jeff Schantz said, not entirely in jest, that they treated their design proposal as a dissertation defense. The university also engaged the eminent light designer James Carpenter. As a MacArthur Fellow in 2004, Carpenter formed a relationship with the University of Chicago when he and physicist Sidney Nagel jointly taught a course on the observable properties of light. Around the same time Carpenter designed the dramatic new illumination of the Midway.

"Louis Kahn said that light reveals architecture. I reverse that and say that architecture reveals light," Carpenter explains. As a practical matter, he devises strategies to make the best use of natural light. This is done partly in the interest of conservation, but also, more poetically, to enrich what we perceive in a building. "You'll be able see light change on the building as you walk up and down the street," he said of Eckhardt. "And you'll see it change at different times of the day." Carpenter hopes that his work will not just enhance the beauty of the building but also inspire scientists who work there, perhaps even inform their investigations. More vividly than before, architecture is bridging the gulf between what is quantifiable, as in science, and what is intuitive, as in art.

ECKHARDT will expose the physical sciences to the outside world in this largely transparent building. Natural light will enrich surfaces and define spaces while reducing the need for artificial illumination inside.

To view updated photos of the Eckhardt Center, scan the QR code at left and select "Eckhardt."

AS A SCULPTOR and more recently as a designer of buildings, Jamie Carpenter uses light as others use clay, bringing unexpected sensory dimensions to buildings and streetscapes. For the University of Chicago, Carpenter's New York studio designed Midway Crossings, three luminous paths across the wide pedestrian expanse that bisects the campus. His studio also designed elaborate light effects for the William Eckhardt Research Center, adding drama to a place that its architects have likened to a cathedral of science.

The Dramatic Dimension

THE LIGHT ART OF JAMIE CARPENTER

Befitting a university where interdisciplinarity is bred in the bone, Carpenter is an artist, glassmaker, metallurgist, and master technician. Through the play of light, his work animates surfaces. It also illustrates how his notion of "volumetric light"—the use of light to define space—may be the next horizon in modern architecture.

In Midway Crossings, Carpenter uses illumination to create a more interesting place—even the illusion of a bridge over water. He sees the project as a design to enhance sensations of "movement and time, and how we engage with time as we pass through the landscape."

Carpenter's objective is to make light as poetic as it is functional. In his design for Eckhardt, for example, he began by proposing strategies to increase the amount of natural light entering the building and ways to make the best use of it. Beyond conservation, he uses transparent, translucent, and reflective materials to do what all architects strive to do: to enrich a sense of place.

THE MIDWAY CROSSINGS.
The light bridges of the Crossings appear to float across the Midway Plaisance.

To view a video of Jamie Carpenter discussing his work on campus, scan the QR code at left and select "Jamie Carpenter."

CHAPTER SEVEN

BUILDING IDEAS WITH MODERN ARCHITECTURE

We shape our buildings, and afterwards our buildings shape us.

—WINSTON CHURCHILL

SIGNIFICANT CHANGE CAME TO the University of Chicago at the turn of the millennium. Undergraduate enrollment began to grow steadily. A capital campaign begun in 2000 brought new sources of wealth. By 2006, with the inauguration of Robert J. Zimmer as university president, a small building boom had grown into an architectural renaissance.

JOE AND RIKA MANSUETO LIBRARY
(*pages 114–115*), Murphy/Jahn and Burns and McDonnell, 2011.

THE SOUTH CAMPUS CHILLER PLANT
(*opposite*), Murphy/Jahn and Burns and McDonnell, 2008.

FORM AND FUNCTION IN UTILITIES

It was an exuberant sign of the times that even an air-conditioning facility became an opportunity for great design. Early in the new century, planners began work on the South Campus Chiller Plant, slated to serve the growing campus south of the Midway. As initially conceived by engineers, the plant would consist of state-of-the-art cooling equipment housed in an indifferent brick box. As for the brick box, the university had more ambitious ideas and asked architect Helmut Jahn if he might take on the project and give it some flair.

THE WEST CAMPUS COMBINED UTILITY PLANT (*above left*), Murphy/Jahn and Burns and McDonnell, 2010, and the South Campus Chiller Plant (*above right*) have won numerous architectural awards.

To view a video of Helmut Jahn discussing his award-winning utility plants, scan the QR code at left and select "Helmut Jahn–Utility Plants."

An architect of unmatched creativity, Jahn was already at work on a new library for the university. Yet he jumped at the chance to design a utility plant that would be a novel essay in structural expression. His concept, characteristically unconventional, was not to hide the equipment inside the plant but to celebrate it. Thus the building has curtain walls of remarkable transparency, made of low-emission, low-reflectivity glass. Air intakes and exhausts operate behind perforated stainless steel panels, which reinforce the appearance of a minimalist, elegantly simple structure.

The South Campus Chiller Plant gained iconic status when it won design awards after its completion in 2008. Two years later Jahn finished the West Campus Combined Utility Plant on the northwest edge of campus, and the clear message of that building was the same: the university was conscientious about energy conservation, exhibiting chillers, pumps, and other equipment in bright colors, and equally committed to advanced architecture. The two went together.

INNOVATIVE DESIGN FOR A NEW ERA

With a reputation for making engineering prominent in architectural design, Jahn and his firm applied their *modus operandi* in a building that served another indispensable function

JOE + RIKA MANSUETO LIBRARY

JOE AND RIKA MANSUETO LIBRARY

of the university. The Joe and Rika Mansueto Library, completed in 2011 and connected to the Regenstein Library by a bridge, advances the idea of a research library several steps into the future. What one sees is a low, elliptical, glass-paneled dome. What one does not see, and can only imagine, is the high-density book storage in the ground beneath the dome.

The planning for Mansueto began the way it did for all great buildings on campus: through intense collaboration. "At Chicago, nothing gets done in a superficial way," says Judith Nadler, director of the university library system. She and a faculty-staff committee began the planning process by selecting five distinguished architecture firms to interview

THE INTRICATE GEOMETRY
of the Mansueto Library interior.

To view a video of Helmut Jahn discussing Mansueto Library, scan the QR code at left and select "Helmut Jahn–Mansueto."

for the project. Librarians at other universities had responded to the digital revolution largely by moving books to off-site storage. Nadler and her group instead were determined to incorporate state-of-the-art library technology—including an automated storage and retrieval system with robotic cranes retrieving the books—while also keeping the original sources on campus.

But how would the components of the new facility be arranged? And how would they fit on such a small site that was located so close to buildings from another era? The committee put these questions to Jahn, and in devising a solution to house the books underground, he drew deeply from an integration of architecture and engineering that he calls "archi-neering."

Jahn's global reputation is based on his ability to employ and expose daring construction technologies in design. Early in this process, Jahn's team had proposed placing the library's robotic system largely underground—making it the first such project

of its kind. But well before developing the scheme, he needed to make sure of the librarians' assent. "If I invest in you, will you invest in me?" he asked Nadler. She replied that she would, and the process involved client and architect in equal measure.

The idea of an elongated glass dome might seem counterintuitive amid the turrets and stone towers of nearby buildings. But the library reflects Jahn's singular ability to introduce contrasting forms that do not jar the senses. Visually, the framing of the dome is rigorously geometric (modernism's pervasive connection with Gothic architecture). Users of the library, with a solar-control glass ceiling overhead, have rapid access to up to 3.5 million volume equivalents underneath via robotic retrieval. Though futuristic, the reading room recalls other magnificent interiors, like Harper Library and Hutchinson Commons, that leave indelible impressions of the University of Chicago.

BUSINESS OF SPACE AND LIGHT

When architects speak of courage, they usually refer to the backbone required to propose and execute a design that no one has created before. The Charles M. Harper Center, campus home of the Booth School of Business, is a salient example. Uruguayan architect Rafael Viñoly displayed unrestrained audacity in designing this angular, light-filled glass complex. When one considers the building's location, near two of the most famous works of architecture on campus, his courage becomes especially apparent.

Earlier campus plans proposed siting the graduate business school south of the Midway, where space and famous neighbors were not at issue. But the school's leadership resisted, largely because Booth's faculty relies on proximity to colleagues in other fields—such as computation, economics, and sociology—working in or near the old quads. Ultimately, the decision was made to locate the business school at 58th Street and Woodlawn Avenue, in a site then occupied by Woodward Court, a 1960 dormitory complex designed by Eero Saarinen. (It would take courage to remove a Saarinen building as well.)

As Viñoly's design developed, faculty who worked with him made long lists of practical requirements, such as smart classrooms, spacious (even gala) meeting facilities, and other interior spaces "to foster collaboration among students and faculty," as Dean Edward Snyder put it when the building was being completed. One architectural challenge would be to create a quiet setting for professors' offices and yet a creatively interactive environment for students.

In some ways the building accomplishes these objectives by using the conventions of corporate architecture, which has aspired of late to transparency and high drama. In Harper Center a great central atrium fills the building with sunlight from top to bottom and end to end. Around three sides of this indoor courtyard, the interior is organized into five stories, with balconies and floating stairways conveying a sense of importance and power.

The corporate analogy goes only so far, however. This unabashedly modern building is surrounded on three sides by Gothic structures—the Lab Schools, Ida Noyes Hall, and Rockefeller Chapel—and on the fourth by Frank Lloyd Wright's Robie House. To blend in as much as possible with all of them, Viñoly assembled the building like a puzzle. On 58th Street, the center's horizontal profile echoes the proportions of the prairie style Robie. In a nod to the Gothic aesthetic, the atrium's soaring supports converge into arches, which recall the groined vaults of the chapel across Woodlawn.

These and other gestures appear forthright, even blunt. Yet creating a contemporary, coherent building that fits in with a timeless campus also requires a subtle touch. Viñoly said that he was proudest of the elements of the design that are almost invisible, such as "the manipulation of scales: how you go from a relatively small room to a large space." These are things that "people may not see," he said, "and that's actually good."

CHARLES M. HARPER CENTER
of the Booth School of Business
(*above and right*), Rafael Viñoly Architects, 2004.
In the Harper Center, Viñoly created immense
spaces and intimate ones. The building
respectfully references its neighbors, with
horizontal lines recalling Robie House and vaulted
interiors echoing the Gothic. A view from the
roof of the Harper Center (*pages 124–125*)
shows Rockefeller Chapel to the west.

To view a video of Rafael Viñoly
discussing the Harper Center,
scan the QR code at left and
select "Rafael Viñoly–Harper."

DESIGN OF A RICHER COMMUNITY

Besides the Mansueto Library and Harper Center, other recent architecture on campus has been guided by many different hands. During the long deanship of Professor John W. Boyer, much-needed improvements to undergraduate life have addressed objectives that had gone unfulfilled since the 1920s.

Modern efforts to upgrade the campus for undergraduates began in earnest in the 1980s, when a faculty committee advocated "campus consolidation" in "the long-term interests of the university and the neighborhood." These efforts, however, took time to bear fruit. In the 1990s, students were still living in converted apartment houses interspersed throughout Hyde Park. But when Boyer became dean of the college in 1992, he began efforts to bring the center of student life to the campus.

The Gerald Ratner Athletics Center was one product of the new emphasis on a campus community, but it was mildly controversial before it opened in 2003. "There were people who said, 'We're not about [sports], that's not who we are,'" remembers law professor and former provost Geoffrey R. Stone, who was on the building committee at the time. Supporters countered that a sports complex was essential to attract the kind of students who could choose between Chicago and other top-flight institutions.

The university hired César Pelli, who worked for Eero Saarinen early in his career, to design the Ratner Center. The commission was awarded less on the basis of a specific drawing or proposal than on Pelli's willingness to discuss many objectives for the project. The university hoped that the building would serve as more than a gym and a pool.

Pelli agreed and explained that he saw 55th Street as an important but largely neglected entry to the campus. Instead of a gate or arch at this outer edge of the university, entryways could be defined instead by activity. An athletics facility was a natural center of interest, and the Ratner Center's design would draw attention—particularly at night, when fritted glass provided inviting views of the interior. More dramatically, the building would be held up by a mast-and-cable system rising sixty feet over an undulating roof.

At around the same time, the university made a leap of faith by hiring Ricardo Legorreta for new dormitories, the Max Palevsky Residential Commons, completed in 2002. Introduced to the university by trustee Thomas Pritzker, whose family founded the Pritzker Architecture Prize (which had included Legorreta as a juror), Legorreta had never designed a building as far north as Chicago. The challenge for the Mexican architect would be to apply his love of simple geometry and bright color—preferences born of his native Mexico—in a climate and tradition so different from his own.

Before beginning to design the sprawling dorm, Legorreta spent weeks wandering the campus and Hyde Park, taking in the environment. He became enchanted with the masonry houses of the neighborhood, and fixed on the brightest brick extant as the dominant tone for the new complex. The colors drew early criticism, as did even brighter pastel-colored entries, which seemed to clash with the limestone all around. But the architecture grew on people. The bright brick amplifies sunlight, especially in the cold, gray months of winter. The courtyards enliven an area that was previously dead space between other buildings. The blending of the new with the old is hardly literal; rather, the dormitories reflect the scale, massing, and geometric rigor of Gothic buildings nearby, while looking nothing like them. The modern dorms have new exterior spaces that blend gracefully with the old, and the dorms' design brings a touch of semitropical radiance to Hyde Park.

ARTISTICALLY CROSSING THE MIDWAY

Ratner and Palevsky made the University of Chicago a more outgoing place, adding to its intellectual energy a more varied and vibrant social life. Another important change

MAX PALEVSKY RESIDENTIAL COMMONS, Ricardo Legorreta, 2002. The color and massing of this sprawling complex are unlike anything else on a campus dominated by gray limestone. But its geometric patterns dovetail with nearby buildings, which range from Gothic revival to midcentury modern.

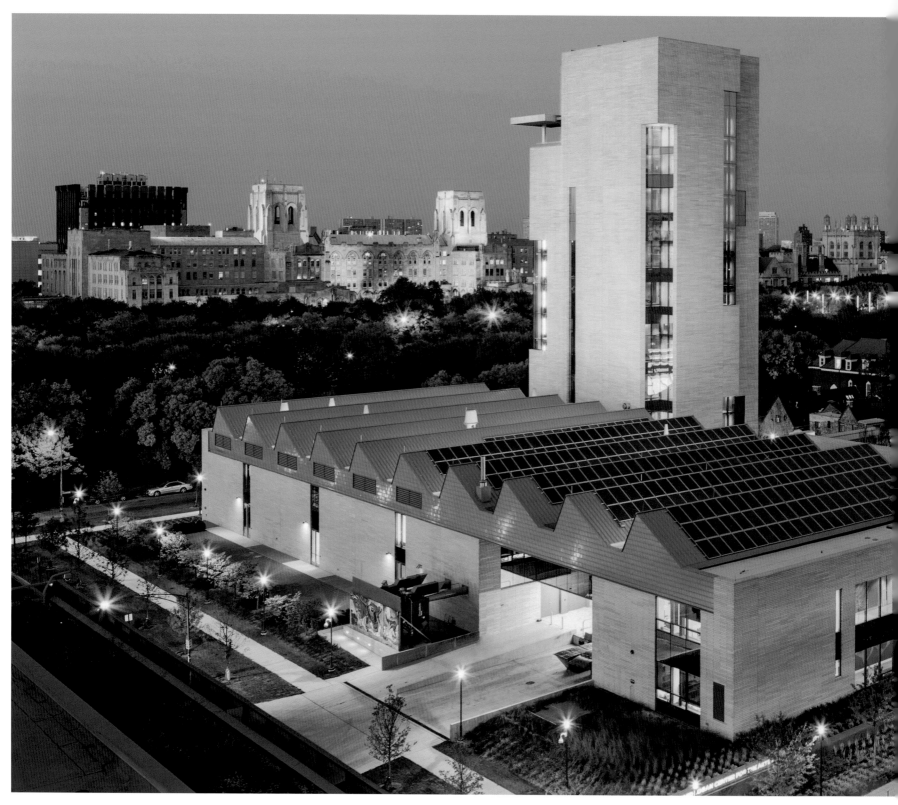

REVA AND DAVID LOGAN CENTER FOR THE ARTS (*pages 130–131, above, and opposite*), Tod Williams Billie Tsien Architects, 2012. The tower of the Logan Center draws attention to the south edge of the Midway. Its high-rise design also provides views of campus and the city beyond.

to the campus came with efforts to connect the north and south sides of the Midway visually and architecturally.

The Midway Plaisance, a parkway that bisects the campus, had been seen as a liability for decades. Changing this required time and a number of interventions, including the creation of three virtual bridges (walkways above the park at Dorchester, Woodlawn, and Ellis Avenues). This became light-master James Carpenter's first design commission on a campus where illumination was increasingly integral to architecture. Across the Midway, lighting was used to create comfort and spark interest in a crossing that previously lacked both.

Among destinations on the southern side of the now well-traveled Midway, the South Campus Residence Hall (as named when new) achieves the kind of south-of-the-Midway presence that the university has long sought. While tall and even imposing, it also enjoys a human scale wrought by being designed emphatically from the inside out. Large enough to house eight hundred undergraduates, it is divided into intimate "houses" with entries, dorm rooms, apartments, and lounges constructed as if (like the quadrangles across the Midway) by accretion. With a solid limestone base and glassy towers reaching

To view a video of Tod Williams and Billie Tsien discussing the Logan Center, scan the QR code at left and select "TWBTA."

eight stories, the exterior appears heedless of symmetry and—also like the Gothic precincts of old—forms a maze of interesting spaces.

Tall buildings have long been missing from the south edge of the Midway. That was one factor that the firm of Tod Williams Billie Tsien Architects considered in their design of the Reva and David Logan Center for the Arts, completed in 2012. As a place for classrooms, public performance, and exhibitions, Logan was envisioned as a transformative project for the campus, its tower marking a public entrance to the university for the South Side community.

Visually, Logan represents an abstract sculpture writ large. Its eleven stories, clad in horizontal limestone slabs, have a sense of weight, compression, and permanence. Yet the mass of the building is pierced by large glass openings and cantilevered protrusions, details that indicate human activity, and plenty of it, going on inside.

The architects readily admit that Logan's complex of studios, galleries, and performance spaces would have been simpler to design closer to the ground. Yet its vertical orientation gives this corner of campus the new life that the university sought. The high rise draws the eye away from the distant main quads, while its upper stories afford unmatched views of those quads. The interior is endlessly varied, with working studios and performance spaces assembled, stacked, and connected by balconies, catwalks, atriums, and green roofs.

"We wanted to claim back the public spaces, which were so glorious and wonderful in older buildings," says Tsien. Thus the halls are wide, the vestibules brightly colored. Stairways have windows and places where you can admire the view; indeed, Williams claims that nothing inspired him in this design quite like the stairways. "They force you to have a sense of where you are," he explains.

Logan's design forces you to have a sense of place not only in space but in time as well. It is a new building situated on an old campus. With its limestone walls, its site on the Midway, its height, and its complex interior circulation, it establishes like no other building on campus the connection—the continuities—between the university's rich past and its soaring ambitions for the future.

THE SEMINARY CO-OP BOOKSTORE,
renovation, Tigerman McCurry Architects, 2012.

ARTS INCUBATOR,
renovation, Built Form, 2013.

To view updated construction
photos and a video of Ann Beha
discussing the renovation of the
Hall for Economics, scan the QR
code at left and select "Ann Beha."

"**NEW IDEAS NEED OLD BUILDINGS**" was how the great urbanist Jane Jacobs expressed her core belief in architectural preservation.

Few projects demonstrate that principle quite like 5757 South University Avenue, the former Chicago Theological Seminary. Built largely in 1923, it was, for over half a century, home to the Seminary Co-op Bookstore. In late 2012, the bookstore moved to renovated space in the University of Chicago's McGiffert House, formerly a CTS dormitory. Designed by the renowned architects at Tigerman McCurry, the playful, repurposed space maintains the character of the co-op while providing more square footage, more sunlight, and more visibility in the neighborhood.

New Ideas and Old Buildings

ADAPTIVE REUSE AT THE UNIVERSITY OF CHICAGO

The space formerly housing the bookstore is now occupied by the Hall for Economics. Ann Beha's Boston-based firm has led this adaptive reuse project. She has said that to her, "there is no greater part of practice than how we treat our heritage."

This balance between the past and present, between preservation and renovation, can also be seen in the university's Arts and Public Life Initiative, directed by artist Theaster Gates. One of its programs, the Arts Incubator in Washington Park, is housed in a renovated 1920s building, a two-story, terra-cotta structure located at Garfield Boulevard and Prairie Avenue, just west of the university's main campus. The wide-open space, punctuated by colorful Art Nouveau details and rich, repurposed woods, has been designed to enhance collaboration among university faculty and students and the arts community in Washington Park by providing space and resources for artists, youth, and members of the community.

THE HALL FOR ECONOMICS, renovation, Ann Beha Architects, expected completion 2014.

EPILOGUE

SINCE ITS FOUNDING IN 1890, the University of Chicago has been a home for the life of the mind. From students at the Lab School to the most distinguished scientists and scholars, people explore, discover, innovate, and grow here, and a spirit of inquiry sets the stage for imagining and disseminating great ideas.

The founders of the University of Chicago understood the importance of the built environment. They knew it would make a strong statement about the character of the university and signal to the world what kind of place this would be. When they adopted Gothic architecture, they instantly conveyed the sense of history, seriousness, and intellectual fortitude found at universities such as Oxford and Cambridge.

As the campus grew, the university continued to view architecture as a powerful force for shaping interaction and building community. Design and site decisions took into consideration the connection between the intellectual and the physical and the fact that ideas are made memorable by locating them in space. Entering the reading room of the

LOGAN CENTER courtyard and green roofs.

Joe and Rika Mansueto Library, one senses the expanse of intellectual possibility beneath glass and sky while appreciating the warmth of wood floors and furniture that grounds one to earth. Embarking on a journey of creative discovery in the Reva and David Logan Center for the Arts, one hears the echo of music while glimpsing the creation of art within studio spaces. Architectural images spark the imagination, connecting the physical and intellectual worlds throughout campus.

Today the University of Chicago is in the midst of a historic transformation. In the first two decades of the twenty-first century, the number of buildings that have been built or are under construction represent 40 percent as many buildings as were constructed during the entire prior history of the university. It is our challenge, responsibility, and aspiration to carry out this expansion in the service and spirit of the university's education and research mission.

To make the most of this period of transformation, we have identified four design principles that are deeply tied to the university's core values.

Foremost is the creation of buildings and spaces that promote the exchange of ideas. We aim to design settings that encourage interaction among faculty, students, and others across disciplines and at multiple levels, from laboratory to ground-floor café to the next green quadrangle.

Second is the stewardship of historically significant spaces and places. While any campus should accommodate growth and change, new interventions can enhance the rich context of the existing environment and be designed with flexibility to imagine the needs of future generations.

Third is a commitment to improving environmental sustainability through the design and operation of all physical resources. The act of building and operating many millions of square feet in the Chicago climate is unavoidably resource intensive but can be done in a way that is responsible and considerate of human health, locally and globally.

Finally, there is the need to continually strengthen the identity and character of our distinctive campus. The values, ethos, and culture of the University of Chicago, vigorously debated and passionately protected, are made tangible in limestone and landscape, glass and garden, portals and pathways.

To view a video of Steve Wiesenthal discussing the university's architecture, scan the QR code at left and select "Steve Wiesenthal."

The university has maintained a tradition of architectural innovation and quality in the hands of notable architects, ranging from Henry Ives Cobb to Rafael Viñoly, from Bertram Grosvenor Goodhue to Eero Saarinen, from Ludwig Mies van der Rohe to Ricardo Legorreta, from Walter Netsch to Helmut Jahn, and many others past and present. The result is a diverse layering of architectural and landscape materials, attitudes, and ideas about what makes an exceptional campus.

As a place conceived for the vibrant exchange of ideas—a home for the life of the mind—the University of Chicago campus will never be finished. Complete, yes, but just as new ideas continually spring forth from students and scholars, the campus will continue to evolve and renew itself.

—STEVE WIESENTHAL, FAIA

Associate Vice President and
University Architect
The University of Chicago

ACKNOWLEDGMENTS

GLASS GOTHIC-INSPIRED ARCHES
train the eye upward in Harper Center's
Rothman Winter Garden.

Building Ideas was inspired by the expansion of the University of Chicago campus
that began at the turn of the twenty-first century. This growth was accompanied by a
succession of architectural triumphs, and one objective in telling the story of the campus
was to reach back to the original ideas of the founders and demonstrate how their work
continued to inform the design of buildings more than a century later. In helping the
author understand the university's long and rich arc of history, Neil Harris, Preston and
Sterling Morton Professor of History and Art History Emeritus, was generous with his
time and insightful about the objectives of the book.

Building Ideas was made possible by the generosity of University of Chicago alumnus
and trustee David Rubenstein, JD '73. Mr. Rubenstein's support and advocacy are visible in
programs and initiatives across the campus as well as in this panoramic tribute.

Tom Rossiter of Chicago brought tirelessness and a remarkably keen eye to the
photography. The splendor of the book is in many ways a credit to his work and vision.

At the University of Chicago Press, editorial director Paul Schellinger's indispensable role was to develop the book's content from idea to realization. Design and production were undertaken by Lisa Lytton and Bea Jackson. Their invaluable experience shaped the book. Editor Leslie Keros provided a critical eye and ear in refining the text and focusing its message. University Communications senior project manager Carmen Marti coordinated the writing, photographing, editing, and designing stages of the book; she remained a crucial presence throughout the process. Nora Semel and Becky Wood were trusted advisors, and Grant Schexnider and Colleen Newquist provided valuable assistance.The project could not have been completed without Information Center interns Alida Miranda-Wolff, Miranda Cherkas, and Jen Wells-Qu.

Steve Wiesenthal, associate vice president and university architect, was generous with his time and expertise throughout the creation of *Building Ideas*. Thanks also to Steve's colleagues in the Facilities Services department: Richard Bumstead, associate director for campus environment; Alicia Murasaki, executive director of planning and design; and Bethany Minton, executive assistant. Former university planner Calvert Audrain was kind in reconstructing past planning decisions and their effect on the campus today. Leann Paul, project consultant for the construction of Harper Center, assisted in telling the story of the Booth School of Business's dramatic new building. Hyde Park author Devereux Bowly shared his encyclopedic knowledge of the community around the campus.

At the University of Chicago Library, thanks to Judith Nadler, director and university librarian; to Dan Meyer, director of the Department of Special Collections; and to Dan's colleagues, Leah Richardson, Eileen Ielmini, Julia Gardner, Christine Colburn, and Judith Dartt.

The author received invaluable assistance from several faculty members: Douglas G. Baird, Harry A. Bigelow Distinguished Service Professor of Law; John W. Boyer, Martin A. Ryerson Distinguished Service Professor in History and Dean of the College; Geoffrey R. Stone, Edward H. Levi Distinguished Service Professor of Law; and John Huizinga, Walter David "Bud" Fackler Distinguished Service Professor of Economics.

Many architects and their colleagues were generous in describing and helping analyze their work for the university: Jamie Carpenter and Ben Colebrook, of James Carpenter Design Associates; Kent Cooper, formerly of Eero Saarinen and Associates and later architect of the addition to the D'Angelo Law Library; Bill Odell, of HOK; Jeff Schantz, formerly of HOK; Dass Mabe and Stacey Williams, of Zimmer Gunzul Frasca; Helmut Jahn, of Murphy/Jahn; Scott Pratt, formerly of Murphy/Jahn and currently of Krueck and Sexton; Mark Hirons, of Cannon Design; and Phil Enquist, of SOM.

—JAY PRIDMORE

SOURCES

Page numbers in text appear in left column.

FOREWORD

xix *"The university has done more"*: Robert F. Herrick, "The University of Chicago," *Scribner's Magazine*, October 1895, 399.

CHAPTER 1. IDEAS AND ARCHITECTURE

3 *"The University of Chicago originated"*: Robert J. Zimmer, address at civic dinner marking his assumption of the presidency of the University of Chicago, September 14, 2006, http://president.uchicago.edu/page/civic-dinner-remarks.

7 *"Florence of the West"*: Theodore Dreiser, *The Titan* (New York: John Lane, 1914), 6.

7 *"The flames swept away forever"*: *Industrial Chicago* (Chicago: Goodspeed Publishing Company, 1891), 1:115, quoted in Carl Condit, *The Chicago School of Architecture* (Chicago: University of Chicago Press, 1964), 19.

7 *"a great college"*: *A Retrospective View of the University of Chicago on the Occasion of Its Centennial: One in Spirit* (Chicago: University of Chicago, 1991), 3. The story of the university's religious origins, John D. Rockefeller's interest in the Baptists' plan, and the hiring of William Rainey Harper to lead the new university draws from this book.

8 *"Do not on account of scarcity"*: Calvert W. Audrain, William B. Cannon, and William B. Wolff, "A Review of Planning at the University of Chicago, 1891–1978," *University of Chicago Record*, April 1978, 47.

10 *The winning proposal:* Details about Cobb, Hutchinson, and Ryerson's early creation of the campus are drawn from Edward Wolner, *Henry Ives Cobb's Chicago: Architecture, Institutions, and the Making of a Modern Metropolis* (Chicago: University of Chicago Press, 2011), 181–244; and Thomas Wakefield Goodspeed, *A History of the University of Chicago: The First Quarter-Century* (1916; Chicago: University of Chicago Press, 1973), 187–213.

10 *"selected as far as possible"*: Charles Jenkins, "The University of Chicago," *Architectural Record*, January 1904, 229–46.

10 *"struck Gothic notes of permanence"*: Jean Block, *The Uses of Gothic: Planning and Building the Campus of the University of Chicago, 1892–1932* (Chicago: University of Chicago Press, 1983), 36.

11 *"the disjointed grotesqueries"*: Thorstein Veblen, *The Higher Learning in America* (New York: B. W. Huebsch, 1918), 146.

11 *"an American University"*: Frank Lloyd Wright, *Modern Architecture: Being the Kahn Lectures for 1930* (1931; Princeton, N.J.: Princeton University Press, 2008), 10.

13 *"a beautiful, harmonious visual picture"*: Eero Saarinen, "Campus Planning: The Unique World of the University," *Architectural Record*, November 1960, 127.

CHAPTER 2. THE GOTHIC CAMPUS

19 *"The choice of Gothic for the University"*: Jean Block, *The Uses of Gothic: Planning and Building the Campus of the University of Chicago, 1892–1932* (Chicago: University of Chicago Press, 1983), 8–13.

MANSUETO LIBRARY epitomizes the university's move toward glass and steel architecture that harmonizes with its Gothic origins.

19 *Like the other architects:* The conditions under which Cobb designed the campus are chronicled in Edward Wolner, *Henry Ives Cobb's Chicago: Architecture, Institutions, and the Making of a Modern Metropolis* (Chicago: University of Chicago Press, 2011), 181–213.

20 *"absolutely independent choice":* Ibid., 191.

20 *"The very latest English Gothic":* Ibid.

20 *"outrival the East":* "Will Outrival the East: Chicago to Have the Finest Athletic Club in the Country," *Chicago Daily Tribune,* March 23, 1890, 1.

20 *"cultural entrepreneur":* Wolner, *Henry Ives Cobb's Chicago,* 186.

20 *"the Gothic template had long been lauded":* See John Ruskin, *The Nature of Gothic* (London: George Allen, 1892).

22 *"We have haunted his office":* Wolner, *Henry Ives Cobb's Chicago,* 197.

22 *"There is no more important public enterprise":* Silas B. Cobb to the Board of Trustees of the University of Chicago, June 9, 1892, quoted in Thomas W. Goodspeed, "Silas Bowman Cobb," *University Record,* January 1920, 56.

23 *"It has a record":* Goodspeed, "Silas Bowman Cobb."

25 *In 1900, Charles Hutchinson visited Europe:* The work of Shepley, Rutan and Coolidge is described and analyzed in Block, *The Uses of Gothic,* 64–71.

25 *"I am coming home":* Charles Hutchinson to William Rainey Harper, April 4, 1900, quoted in ibid., 67.

27 *In like manner, the university seal:* The seal was adopted by the university trustees in 1912. Ibid., colophon.

31 *Ida Noyes Hall was created:* The story of Ida Noyes Hall is drawn from ibid., 116–23.

31 *"tolerance, sympathy, kindness":* Thomas Wakefield Goodspeed, *A History of the University of Chicago: The First Quarter-Century* (1916; Chicago: University of Chicago Press, 1973), 441.

35 *"we agreed that its beauty . . . appetite for such knowledge":* Edith Foster Flint to Harry Pratt Judson, October 21, 1916, quoted in Block, *The Uses of Gothic,* 123.

35 *To design the chapel:* The story of Rockefeller chapel is told in ibid., 152–61.

37 *"malleable enough to be molded":* Bertram Grosvenor Goodhue, "The Romanticist Point of View," *Craftsman,* April–September 1905, 322.

CHAPTER 3. THE OLMSTED EFFECT

43 *"Its civilizing and humanizing influence":* Andreas Simon, comp. and ed., *Chicago, the Garden City* (Chicago: Franz Gindele Printing Co., 1893), 52, quoted in Victoria Post Ranney, *Olmsted in Chicago* (1972; Chicago: The Field Museum, 1998), 34.

43 *That was the acquisition of the site:* Calvert W. Audrain, William B. Cannon, and William B. Wolff, "A Review of Planning at the University of Chicago, 1891–1978," *University of Chicago Record,* April 1978, 47–51.

43 *"the ideal site":* Thomas Wakefield Goodspeed, *The Story of the University of Chicago: 1890–1925* (Chicago: University of Chicago Press, 1925), 30–32, quoted in Edward Wolner, *Henry Ives Cobb's Chicago: Architecture, Institutions, and the Making of a Modern Metropolis* (Chicago: University of Chicago Press, 2011), 187.

44 *"helped transform a suburban idyll":* Wolner, *Henry Ives Cobb's Chicago,* 194.

47 *Enlightened attitudes also led:* The creation of Washington and Jackson Parks and the Midway Plaisance is chronicled in Ranney, *Olmsted in Chicago*, 25–39.

47 *"It was more like Graceland Cemetery":* Richard Bumstead, interview with author, January 2013.

48 *"corresponding simplicity, formality, and dignity":* William Tippins, "The Olmsted Brothers in the Midwest," *Midwestern Landscape Architecture* (Urbana: University of Illinois Press, 2000), 164.

53 *Then in 1929, an interest:* Beatrix Farrand describes her work at the university in her essay "Squaring the Circle: A Study of Campus Development," *University of Chicago Magazine*, June 1936, 3–6.

54 *In 1958, one of Eero Saarinen's first university assignments:* Modernist plans of Saarinen and Barnes are covered in Audrain, Cannon, and Wolff, "A Review of Planning," 59–74. Saarinen discusses his university plans in his essay "Campus Planning: The Unique World of the University," *Architectural Record*, November 1960, 123–30. Barnes's plan is further described in "North Quad: A Planned Environment," *Chicago Maroon*, March 8, 1958, 15.

57 *the university's botanic garden is the envy:* Bumstead, interview with author.

57 *"they are one and the same":* Ibid.

CHAPTER 4. AN EXPANDING ENTERPRISE

63 *"It is the best investment":* University Record, July 1896, 223.

64 *"Bran splinter new":* Robert Maynard Hutchins, *The Higher Learning in America* (New Haven, CT: Yale University Press, 1936), xiv.

64 *When Harper was preparing to leave:* The most recent biography of Breasted is Jeffrey Abt, *American Egyptologist: The Life of James Henry Breasted and the Creation of His Oriental Institute* (Chicago: University of Chicago Press, 2011).

65 Time *magazine pictured:* "Science," *Time*, December 14, 1931, 23–24.

66 *This was the medical complex:* The origins of the medical school and the Harper-Rockefeller controversy are chronicled in F. Howell Wright, *Reminiscences of the Bobs Roberts Memorial Hospital: The Growth and Development of a Department of Pediatrics* (Chicago: University of Chicago, 1990), 3. This work is available in the Department of Special Collections, Joseph Regenstein Library.

68 *"The preservation of the highest ideals":* James Angell, "Medicine and the University," *University Record*, January 1928, 17–25.

68 *"Sunlight is now an acknowledged retardant":* John Allan Hornsby and Richard E. Schmidt, *The Modern Hospital: Its Inspiration; Its Architecture; Its Equipment; Its Operation* (Philadelphia: W.B. Saunders Co., 1913), 34.

69 *"We like to believe":* Frederic C. Woodward, *The President's Report Covering the Academic Year July 1, 1926–June 30, 1927* (Chicago: University of Chicago Press, 1928), 3–4, quoted in John W. Boyer, *"The Kind of University That We Desire to Become": Student Housing and the Educational Mission of the University of Chicago*, Occasional Papers of Higher Education, no. 18 (Chicago: College of the University of Chicago, 2008), 50.

70 *Architect Charles Z. Klauder of Philadelphia:* The story of student housing in the college is drawn from Boyer, "The Kind of University," 52–58.

70 *"Let undergraduate loafers go":* William E. Dodd to Bessie Louise Pierce, February 3, 1934, Bessie Louise Pierce Papers, box 9, folder 10, Special Collections Research Center, University of Chicago Library, quoted in ibid., 60.

72 *Around the turn of the century:* The history of the Laboratory Schools is drawn from William Harms and Ida DePencier, *Experiencing Education: 100 Years of Learning at the University of Chicago Laboratory Schools* (Chicago: University of Chicago Laboratory Schools, 1996).

72 *"a well defined retired character":* James Gamble Rogers, "The Architecture of the School of Education Building," *University Record*, November 1903, 184.

72 *Sunny Gymnasium, built in 1929:* John P. Howe, "Five Years of Building," *University of Chicago Magazine*, July–August 1929, 511.

73 *Intended to meet a long-standing need:* On the consolidation of administrative offices, see Jeannette Lowrey, "News of the Quadrangles: The New Administration Building," *University of Chicago Magazine*, October 1946, 15. On the preference of modernist design over Gothic, see Herbert P. Zimmermann, "The Administration Building: An Official Interpretation," *University of Chicago Magazine*, January 1947, 10; William V. Morgenstern, "One Man's Opinion: Speaking of Gothic . . . ," *University of Chicago Magazine*, December 1947, 7–8.

75 *The university magazine complained:* Morgenstern, "One Man's Opinion," 7.

75 *Early credit for the anti-Gothic style:* The story of the Administration Building is drawn from Carroll Mason Russell, *The University of Chicago and Me: 1901–1962* (Chicago: privately printed, 1982), 83–84.

75 *"I shall never forget":* Girard T. Bryant, letter to the editor, *University of Chicago Magazine*, December 1946, 1.

75 *"so as to conceal":* W. A. McDermid, letter to the editor, *University of Chicago Magazine*, December 1946, 1.

CHAPTER 5. EMBRACING MIDCENTURY MODERNISM

81 *"Universities are to our time":* *Eero Saarinen on His Work* (New Haven, CT: Yale University Press, 1962), 124.

81 *"The battle of modern architecture has been won":* Eero Saarinen, "Campus Planning: The Unique World of the University," *Architectural Record*, November 1960, 125.

83 *"Always look at the next larger thing":* Ibid., 130.

83 *"Imagine what would have happened":* Ibid., 127.

84 *"The law faculty didn't feel":* Kent Cooper, interview with author, October 2012.

85 *"express in our architecture":* Saarinen, "Campus Planning," 129.

91 *For Joseph Regenstein Library, completed in 1970:* The early life of the Regenstein and its nickname the "quiet giant" come from "Regenstein Library: A Quiet Giant," *Chicago Maroon*, March 8, 1968, 11–13.

92 *"not dominate the area . . . negative spaces":* Ibid., 13.

92 *"What was important to me":* Walter Netsch, interview by Betty J. Blum, June 5–28, 1995, transcript, p. 138, Chicago Architects Oral History Project, Ryerson and Burnham Libraries, Art Institute of Chicago, http://digital-libraries.saic.edu/cdm/compoundobject/collection/caohp/id/19289/rec/1.

92 *"The Gothic form":* Ibid.

92 *"Kids, don't try this at home":* Anders Nereim, "What Is Netsch's Field Theory?" *Inland Architect*, May–June 1990, 64–65.

93 *Regenstein might have done that too:* Calvert W. Audrain, interview with author, October 2005.

CHAPTER 6. THE ARCHITECTURE OF SCIENCE

99   *"Laboratory buildings are like Gothic cathedrals"*: Jeff Schantz, "Architecture + Science = Environment" panel discussion, Argonne and Fermilab Joint Speaker Series, May 19, 2011, http://news.uchicago.edu/multimedia/architecture-science-environment-panel-discussion.

101   *"A century ago there was really"*: William Rainey Harper, *The Trend in Higher Education* (Chicago: University of Chicago Press, 1905), 49.

101   *"I have believed that moral evils"*: Thomas Wakefield Goodspeed, *A History of the University of Chicago: The First Quarter-Century* (1916; Chicago: University of Chicago Press, 1973), 306.

102   *Professors George Marmont and Robert Moon:* "Desiderata for a Space to House a Community of Scientists," May 23, 1946, Buildings and Grounds Records, box 49, folder 3, Department of Special Collections, Joseph Regenstein Library, University of Chicago.

102   *"One might think of the lower part"*: David H. Katzive, "Henry Moore's Nuclear Energy: The Genesis of a Monument," *Art Journal* 32, no. 3 (1973): 286, quoted in *Henry Moore: Writings and Conversations*, ed. Alan Wilkinson (Berkeley: University of California Press, 2002), 293.

103   *"Modern architecture has always denied"*: I. W. Colburn, undated pamphlet (ca. 1968), Architecture and Design reference files, Department of Special Collections, Lake Forest College, Lake Forest, IL.

109   *"money spent on architecture"*: Gary Van Zandbergen, "Architecture + Science = Environment" panel discussion.

111   *"create environments that are evermore"*: Steve Wiesenthal, ibid.

111   *"Louis Kahn said that light reveals architecture . . . times of the day"*: James Carpenter, interview with author, March 2013.

CHAPTER 7. BUILDING IDEAS WITH MODERN ARCHITECTURE

117   *"We shape our buildings"*: Winston Churchill, speech before the House of Commons, October 28, 1943.

119   *"At Chicago, nothing gets done in a superficial way"*: Jay Pridmore, "Make No Little Quads," *University of Chicago Magazine*, May–June 2009, 34.

121   *"If I invest in you"*: Ibid.

121   *"to foster collaboration among students and faculty"*: *Architectural Record*, October 2002, quoted in Anthony Ruth, "Chicago GSB Hyde Park Center Makes Headlines," *Chicago Booth Magazine*, Summer/Fall 2004, 13.

122   *"the manipulation of scales . . . that's actually good"*: Anthony Ruth, "'A Sense of Unified Purpose,'" *Chicago Booth Magazine*, Summer/Fall 2004, 23.

126   *"campus consolidation" in "the long-term interests"*: Lloyd Rudolph et al., *Report of the Faculty Committee on Student Housing* (Archive of the College, November 1983), 20–21, quoted in John W. Boyer, "*The Kind of University That We Desire to Become*": *Student Housing and the Educational Mission of the University of Chicago*, Occasional Papers of Higher Education, no. 18 (Chicago: College of the University of Chicago, 2008), 107.

127   *"There were people who said"*: Geoffrey Stone, interview with author, October 2005.

133   *"We wanted to claim back"*: Billie Tsien, lecture at opening of Reva and David Logan Center for the Arts, Chicago, IL, October 12, 2012.

133   *"They force you to have"*: Tod Williams, ibid.

INDEX

Page numbers in boldface refer to images and captions.

Photo credits: All images by Tom Rossiter unless otherwise noted.

Pages 5, 8, 10, 23, 31, 42, 64, 66, 70, 101: Special Collections Research Center, University of Chicago Library

Pages 102, 110: AJSNY; Page 135: Dbox, New York; Pages 14, 108, 109: Andrew Bruah

Text for this book is set in Verdigris, designed by Mark van Bronkhurst in 2003.

Captions and other details are set in various weights of Gotham, designed by H&FJ in 2000.

The decorative initial caps are set in Fette Fraktur, designed by Johann Christian Bauer in 1850.

Gotham and Fette Fraktur Black are two of the signature fonts for the University of Chicago.